Samuel French Acting Edition

God's Favorite

by Neil Simon

FOR PRODUCTION INQUIRIES

UNITED STATES AND CANADA
info@concordtheatricals.com
1-866-979-0447

UNITED KINGDOM AND EUROPE
licensing@concordtheatricals.co.uk
020-7054-7200

Each title is subject to availability from Concord Theatricals Corp., depending upon country of performance. Please be aware that GOD'S FAVORITE may not be licensed by Concord Theatricals Corp. in your territory. Professional and amateur producers should contact the nearest Concord Theatricals Corp. office or licensing partner to verify availability.

MUSIC AND THIRD PARTY MATERIALS USE NOTE

IMPORTANT BILLING AND CREDIT REQUIREMENTS

GOD'S FAVORITE was first presented on December 11, 1974 by Emanuel Azenberg and Eugene V. Wolsk at the Eugene O'Neill Theatre in New York, New York. The performance was directed by Michael Bennett, with sets by William Ritman, lights by Tharon Musser, and costumes by Joseph G. Aulisi. The cast was as follows:

JOE BENJAMIN . . . . Vincent Gardenia

BEN BENJAMIN . . . . Lawrence John Moss

SARAH BENJAMIN . . . . Laura Esterman

ROSE BENJAMIN . . . . Maria Karnilova

DAVID BENJAMIN . . . . Terry Kiser

MADY . . . . Rosetta LeNoire

MORRIS . . . . Nick LaTour

SIDNEY LIPTON . . . . Charles Nelson Reilly

CHARACTERS

JOE BENJAMIN
BEN BENJAMIN
SARAH BENJAMIN
ROSE BENJAMIN
DAVID BENJAMIN
MADY
MORRIS
SIDNEY LIPTON

SETTING

The action takes place in the Benjamin mansion on the North Shore of Long Island.

TIME

ACT I
Scene One: Midnight.
Scene Two: Two weeks later.

ACT II

The Holocaust after.

To Ellen and Nancy

ACT I

Scene One

(The scene is the palatial home of wealthy businessman **JOE BENJAMIN** *on the North Shore of Long Island Sound. The design of the living room is stylized. It is today, and yet it has a feeling of timelessness. Wooden-beamed ceilings seem to stretch up to heaven itself. An enormous French door leads out to a portico which faces the Sound. A large oak door on one side of the room leads to the entrance foyer. An oak door on the other side leads to the dining room. The walls are adorned with paintings worthy of a collection, which indeed one day they will be. Leather-bound volumes of the great works of literature line the shelves.)*

(Before the curtain rises, we can hear the chiming of a grandfather clock signaling the hour. One...two...three...four...)

(The curtain rises. The room is in darkness. Through the French door, moonlight can be seen reflecting on the snow; it pours an eerie light into the room.)

(The clock continues. Five...six...seven... eight...nine...ten...eleven...twelve. All is silent.)

(Suddenly, a solitary figure is seen outside on the portico. The light is too dim for us to make out his features. He looks around carefully, blows on his hands, then attempts to open the door. It is locked. He blows on his hands again, looks around once more, and tries the door again, but this time using more pressure. The door opens a few inches – but at that very moment, a piercing burglar alarm goes off.)

(The figure pulls away from the door in fear. He seems panicked as he starts to run in three different directions, constantly changing his mind. Finally, in desperation, he jumps over the balcony and disappears from sight. An explosion of snow rises up visibly – he must have landed in a snow bank.)

(The alarm continues its scream. The oak door suddenly swings open. A man enters. He switches on the lights. He is dressed in a rich silk robe, silk pajamas and monogrammed velvet slippers. He reaches behind the shelf and turns off a switch. The alarm stops.)

(This is **JOE BENJAMIN***. In his late fifties, he gives an impression of great strength of character. He glances around the room quickly, giving a fast look behind the drapes. Then he goes over to the French door and notices it is open.)*

(Two more people rush in through the oak door in their night clothes. They are **BEN BENJAMIN** *and* **SARAH BENJAMIN***, a pair of twenty-four-year-old twins, or as close as we can approximate. The brother and sister have red hair of the same shade; their I.Q. is one hundred and sixty – between them.)*

BEN. What is it, Dad? What happened?

JOE. I don't know.

SARAH. What happened, Dad? What is it?

JOE. I said I don't know.

SARAH. We heard the alarm go off.

BEN. Did you hear the alarm go off, Dad?

JOE. Certainly I heard it go off. That's why I'm down here. *(To* **SARAH**.*)* Close your bathrobe.

> *(**SARAH** can never keep her robe tied. She closes it.)*

SARAH. My God, it was really the alarm.

BEN. *(Points.)* The French door is open. Look!

SARAH. It's open, Dad. The French door. Look!

JOE. I can see it's open. Stop repeating everything.

> *(The telephone rings.)*

BEN. It's the phone, Dad.

SARAH. Dad, it's the phone.

> *(It rings again.)*

JOE. I can hear it. Close your bathrobe. Ben, answer the phone.

SARAH. Answer the phone, Ben.

JOE. I'm going to look outside.

SARAH. Suppose someone's out there?

JOE. That's why I'm looking. That's the whole point of it. Close your robe.

> *(The phone rings again.)*

Answer that.

> *(**JOE** goes out to the portico, and **BEN** picks up the phone.)*

BEN. *(Into the phone.)* Hello? ...Yes?

SARAH. Who is it?

BEN. The burglar alarm company.

SARAH. Daddy, it's the burglar alarm company.

BEN. *(Into the phone.)* Yes, we just heard it.

SARAH. Ben said we just heard it.

JOE. *(From out on the portico, yells.)* Close your bathrobe!

BEN. *(Into the phone.)* We found the living-room French door open. My father's checking now.

SARAH. What do they think?

BEN. *(Into the phone.)* What do you think?

JOE. *(Coming back into the room.)* I think someone tried to break in.

BEN. *(Into the phone.)* My father thinks someone tried to break in.

JOE. I found footprints in the snow.

BEN. *(Into the phone.)* He found footprints in the snow.

SARAH. My God, footprints in the snow.

JOE. Close your robe, you want to catch cold? Go to bed. Look at you shivering.

SARAH. I'm not cold. I'm scared. My God, someone tried to break in.

JOE. Stop using God's name in vain.

SARAH. It's not in vain. I'm really scared.

BEN. *(Into the phone.)* One second, please. *(To* **JOE**.*)* They want to know if they should send somebody.

JOE. No one got into the house.

BEN. How can you tell?

JOE. There's snow outside. There would be footprints on the rug.

SARAH. There *are* footprints. *(Points.)* Right there!

JOE. *Those are mine!* Wasn't I just in the snow?

BEN. Suppose he wore galoshes and left them outside?

JOE. What kind of a robber wears galoshes? No one got in. Tell them never mind. Everything's all right. I'm going to look around again.

(He goes back out on the portico.)

BEN. *(Into the phone.)* Hello? No one got in... Never mind, please. Everything's all right. My father's going to look around again... Thank you. We will. *(He hangs up.)* Close your bathrobe.

JOE. *(Comes back in.)* Someone was here. He dropped these outside.

(He holds up a pair of steel-rimmed glasses.)

BEN. Eyeglasses!

SARAH. Look, Daddy, it's a pair of eyeglasses!

JOE. *Didn't I just find them?* I can see they're eyeglasses. Well, whoever dropped them won't get far without them. They're a half-inch thick – I can't see two feet through them.

SARAH. A half-blind burglar, my God, it gives me the creeps.

(She shivers.)

JOE. I'm not going to tell you about God's name or your bathrobe again... I wouldn't be surprised if he broke both his legs. There are no footprints going down the stairs, so he must have jumped off the balcony.

BEN. Jumped off the balcony? Forty feet? He'd break both his legs.

SARAH. Oh God, a crippled blind burglar...

BEN. Why don't we call the police? A crippled blind burglar shouldn't be too hard to find.

JOE. First of all, he isn't a burglar because he didn't steal anything. And second of all, I don't want any police around here with your mother in the house. You know how frightened she is.

BEN. But whoever it was could still be out there. He could be a dangerous lunatic.

SARAH. He could be a rapist! ...A *sexual* rapist!

(She closes her robe, which always falls open.)

BEN. *All* rapists are sexual.

JOE. *(Looks at her.)* He can't see two feet ahead of him, who's he going to find to rape?

SARAH. He could feel his way into the house.

BEN. Not if he has two broken legs.

SARAH. He could *crawl* and feel his way into the house.

JOE. *(Yells.)* People don't break into houses if they have to crawl and feel around... How would they ever get away?

SARAH. A girl in my college was attacked by a man with one arm and one leg... They still can't figure out how he held her down.

JOE. A nineteen-room house with priceless paintings, irreplaceable antiques and a half a million dollars in jewelry, who's going to stop for a rape? He's got other things on his mind.

SARAH. What if rape was the thing he had on his mind?

JOE. Will you stop talking about rape and close your bathrobe? Ben, take her upstairs. Go to bed, the both of you.

SARAH. Yes, Daddy. Good night, Daddy.

BEN. Good night, Dad.

JOE. Wait a minute! Did you just hear something? ...Listen!

> *(We hear a door screech open, then shut. They all look at each other.)*

JOE. It's in the house.

BEN. Someone's in the house!

SARAH. Oh God, the rapist!

JOE. *(Whispers.)* Be quiet! Listen...footsteps!

SARAH. Coming this way!

BEN. Out in the hall!

SARAH. Give them what they want, Daddy, don't let them do you-know-what.

JOE. Get back, both of you. Near the wall!

(They all move back and pin themselves against the wall.)

BEN. The burglar alarm is off. We forgot to reset it.

JOE. It's too late now.

BEN. I could call them. What's the number?

JOE. How should I know the number?

BEN Should I call information?

JOE. Will you get back against the wall?

SARAH. Oh God, I can just feel his hands on me now, his clammy hands rubbing all over me, up and down, up and down –

JOE. No one's going to rub you up and down! Stop it! Grab something!

(They each pick up a vase.)

The minute I hit him, call the police! Stand back! Here he comes... Close your bathrobe!

(They all stand behind the door, and raise the vases over their heads, poised for action – and then the phone rings. They all turn and look at it.)

Now? Now the phone rings?

BEN. What a time for the phone to ring.

JOE. Answer it! Answer it!

*(**BEN** runs over on tiptoe and answers the phone, still speaking in a soft voice.)*

BEN. Hello? ...Yes? ...Yes, this is the Benjamin residence –

JOE. Who is it?

BEN. *(Hand over the receiver, to **JOE**.)* It's a woman. She's asking for Sidney.

JOE. Sidney who?

(The vase is still poised over his head.)

BEN. *(Into the phone.)* Sidney who, please? *(He nods. To **JOE**.)* Sidney Lipton.

JOE. There's no Sidney Lipton here. She's got the wrong number.

BEN. *(Into the phone.)* There's no Sidney Lipton here, madam. You've got the wrong number.

SARAH. Hang up! Stop talking before the rapist goes away.

BEN. *(Into the phone.)* Just a minute. *(To* **JOE**.*)* She says she's *Mrs.* Lipton. Her husband had an appointment here tonight...with you.

> (**JOE** *shakes his head "No" and shrugs,* **BEN**, *back into the phone.)*

My father doesn't know anything about it... Listen, Mrs. Lipton, this is a bad time for us to talk... We're expecting someone... Yes, I will... Thank you.

> *(He hangs up carefully, then rushes back to his spot against the wall. He doesn't say anything,* **JOE** *stares at him.)*

JOE. Yes, you will what?

BEN. Tell Sidney that his wife called.

SARAH. Here he comes!

> *(They all stare at the foyer door. But it is the dining room door that opens, slowly, creaking – and a woman appears. It is* **ROSE BENJAMIN**. *In her early fifties, she wears a silk robe, satin slippers, and tons of jewelry – pearls, rings, earrings, bracelets – a walking Harry Winstons. She walks slowly into the room, not noticing anything yet. Then she turns and sees the three poised against the wall, all with their "weapons" raised in the air. She just looks at them.)*

ROSE. *(Calmly.)* What's wrong?

JOE. *(Innocently.)* Wrong? What could be wrong?

ROSE. What?

JOE. I said, "What could be wrong?"

ROSE. I can't hear you. I have my earplugs in.

JOE. Then take them *out*!

ROSE. I can't hear you. I have my earplugs in.

JOE. *(Yells.)* NOTHING'S WRONG!

ROSE. David's not home yet. I don't like it when David comes home so late. Tell him I want to speak to him in the morning, Joe. All right?

JOE. Yes, Rose. I'll tell him.

ROSE. I can't hear you. I have my earplugs in.

JOE. I'LL TELL HIM!

ROSE. Never mind. You tell him! I'm going to bed. Good night, Joe. Good night, children.

SARAH & BEN. Good night, Mother.

ROSE. You can at least say good night...

(*She turns and exits.*)

JOE. *(Relieved.)* Ahhh!

SARAH & BEN. Ahhh!

JOE. I wonder if that was David?

BEN. *(Puzzled.)* No, Dad. It was Mother.

JOE. *(Frowns at him.)* Not just now. Before. Maybe he came home late again, drunk as usual, forgot his key and tried to get in through the French door.

BEN. That's my guess. That sounds like David.

JOE. All right, let's all go to bed. We've had enough for one night. I'll turn the alarm on.

SARAH. *(Starting out.)* I'll never sleep. I keep picturing some horrid man rubbing his clammy hands all over me, up and down, up and down...

JOE. No one's going to rub you up and down.

(*He turns the lights off and they all leave. The room is empty and dark, except for the moonlight pouring in through the windows. Suddenly a man appears on the portico. He wears a raincoat and a party hat. He wobbles, slightly drunk. He opens the French door and the alarm goes off, screaming through the house. He turns the lights on, then crosses to the other side, removing his raincoat. He wears an expensive tuxedo jacket, silk lace shirt, black tie and, in contrast, filthy, torn blue jeans, with colorful appliques, and old sneakers,* **JOE** *rushes into the room, but he doesn't see* **DAVID***. He dashes to the wall and turns the alarm off. Just as he turns,* **DAVID** *greets him – and* **JOE** *screams in terror.*)

DAVID. Hi, Dad!

JOE. Oh! *(Then, relieved.)* David – so it was you. Thank God!

(Then he slaps at **DAVID***'s shoulders.)*

Bum! Drunken bum! Rotten, good-for-nothing drunken bum!

DAVID. Oh, good. For a minute I thought I was in the wrong house.

BEN. *(Offstage.)* Who is it, Dad?

JOE. It's David, the bum.

*(***SARAH** *and* **BEN** *enter.)*

SARAH. David!

BEN. It's David.

DAVID. Hi, kids. It's David.

JOE. You want to scare us all to death? You want to give the three of us a heart attack?

DAVID. A *triple* heart attack? I don't think it can be done, Dad.

(He wobbles.)

JOE. Look at him! Can't even stand up straight. Thank God your mother can't see you, she's got earplugs on.

DAVID. How does that affect the eyes, Dad?

JOE. Don't you talk back to me… I thought it was a burglar. Your brother thought it was a lunatic. Your sister was expecting a rapist.

DAVID. Sorry, Sarah, what time were you expecting him?

JOE. Go to your room! You hear me? You think you can find your room in your condition?

DAVID. Why should my room be in my condition?

JOE. Get him out! Get him out before I smack him one!

BEN. Cool it, David. Dad is very upset.

(**DAVID** *sits on the end of a fireplace fender.*)

SARAH. Come to bed, David.

JOE. A lot of help you'd be if we had a prowler out there now.

DAVID. *(He points.)* Oh, but we do. I saw something move out there.

(*He falls into the fireplace.*)

JOE. What! Someone's out there? You saw him?

SARAH. And my bathrobe's open.

JOE. *(Looks toward the window.)* I knew it! I knew it!

BEN. Dad knew it! He knew it!

(**DAVID** *goes over to the bottle of Scotch and pours a drink.*)

SARAH. Dad found his glasses on the porch.

BEN. He's probably half blind!

DAVID. Lucky dog!

JOE. GET AWAY FROM THAT LIQUOR!

DAVID. Sorry. Which liquor can I go near?

JOE. You hear?

(*They glare at each other. Suddenly* **MORRIS** *and* **MADY**, *two middle-aged black domestics, appear in the room.*)

MORRIS. Mr. Benjamin.

BEN. Dad, it's Mady and Morris!

DAVID. Looks like Mady and Morris.

MORRIS. Mr. Benjamin, we heard the alarm. Is anything wrong?

JOE. No, no, Morris. It was a mistake.

MORRIS. Mady thought she saw something run past our window before.

MADY. At first I thought it was a dog, but it bumped into a tree. Never saw a dog bump into a tree.

MORRIS. Then she heard it call out in the dark.

JOE. What'd it say, Mady?

MADY. Sounded like "Ohh, my head." Never heard a dog say "Ohh, my head."

JOE. No, no. It was probably just the wind.

MADY. Never heard the wind say "Ohh, my head" either.

JOE. It's nothing. Go back to bed. Don't say anything to Mrs. Benjamin in the morning.

MORRIS. Yes, sir. Good night, Mr. Benjamin.

> *(They start out.)*

MADY. It's gettin' dangerous around here. I don't like livin' in rich neighborhoods.

MORRIS. Come on, Mady.

> *(They go.)*

DAVID. She's right, Dad. Why don't you buy us a nice poor neighborhood so we'd all feel safer?

> *(He takes another drink. **JOE** grabs the glass away from him.)*

JOE. Give me that. How many times have I told you we only drink in this house on holidays and special occasions?

DAVID. If I guess right, can I have a drink?

JOE. *I will not tolerate disrespect!*

DAVID. I mean no disrespect. I apologize, Dad.

JOE. An apology? From you? That's the first one I ever remember.

DAVID. Ahh, a special occasion. That means I can have a drink.

> *(He goes over to the bar.)*

BEN. Come on, David. Let's go to bed.

SARAH. Please don't drink any more, David.

JOE. *(To* **DAVID**.*)* Why can't you be helpful? There's a professional burglar feeling his way around out there someplace... Keep away from this door. I'm going to find out what's going on.

(He opens the French door.)

If he attacks me, call the police and try not to wake your mother.

BEN. Careful, Dad.

SARAH. Be careful, Daddy.

*(***JOE*** goes out on the portico; he pulls his robe collar up. We hear the cold wind blow.)*

BEN. You think it's all right to let him go out there alone?

DAVID. In his bathrobe and slippers? How much money could they get off him?

(He gets his usual from the bar.)

JOE. *(On the portico, calls out in slow, deliberate words... like two ships passing in the fog.)* Hellooo? ...Who's out there? *(Silence.)* What do you want and where do you come from?

DAVID. He expects him to give him his name and address.

(He pours himself one.)

JOE. *(Calling out again.)* What is it you want? ...If you're cold and want a drink, just say so...

DAVID. So *that's* how you get one!

JOE. *(Yelling out.)* Can you see me? I have your glasses in my pocket. If your legs are broken, just crawl up to the house and we'll get you a doctor.

DAVID. *(Drinks.)* And you can pay us back a little bit each week.

SARAH. *(Turns.)* Listen! Someone's coming down the stairs.

BEN. It's Mother. I hear her jewelry.

SARAH. My God, what'll we do? She'll panic.

(The door opens and **ROSE** *reappears, clutching a huge jewel box to her bosom. There are so many jewels crammed into the box that necklaces, pearls and chains are overflowing it.)*

ROSE. *(Quickly, nervously.)* I heard noises. What were the noises? David, is that you? Yes, it's you. Where were you so late? Do you know you had me so worried? Why is everyone here? Is anything wrong? Where's your father? Why isn't your father here? What's happening? What's going on? What's all this about?

DAVID. *(To* **BEN.***)* You answer the first six, I'll take the rest.

BEN. *(To* **DAVID.***)* She can't hear you. She has earplugs in.

ROSE. I can hear you. I don't have my earplugs in. Oh God, I feel weak. My jewel box is so heavy.

JOE. *(Still on the terrace, calls out.)* We know you're out there! Speak up, damnit, I'm losing patience.

ROSE. Who's that? Is that your father? Who's your father talking to?

DAVID. You mustn't worry, Mother. It's not another woman.

JOE. *(Calling out.)* All right, you want to freeze! Freeze!

(He comes back in, and closes the door.)

Let 'em freeze!

ROSE. Who's out there, Joe?

JOE. *(To* **BEN.***)* Can she hear me?

*(***BEN*** nods.)*

No one. No one's out there!

ROSE. You're keeping something from me, all of you. I demand to know what it is. I'm the woman of this house. David, Ben, Sarah, I'm your mother. Joe, I'm your wife.

DAVID. We all know who you are, Mother.

JOE. Rose, please. There's no point in upsetting you.

ROSE. *(She sits.)* I will not get upset. Why does everyone think I always get upset? I'm perfectly capable of handling a situation as long as I know what it is... *Now what is it?*

JOE. Someone was trying to break into the house.

> *(Her head drops as if in a faint – but she never loses her grip on the jewel box.)*

Rose, Rose!

DAVID. *(To the others.)* You see? Why were you so worried about telling her?

JOE. *(Rushes to her, slaps her wrist.)* Rose, are you all right?

ROSE. *(Screams.) Agghh! My jewels!*

JOE. It's me, Rose. Joe – the one who bought the jewels! It's all right.

ROSE. In my house. A burglar in my house.

JOE. *(Yells.)* Okay, that's enough! *That's enough, everybody!* Do you hear me? One little alarm goes off and everybody goes crazy. There is nothing wrong here. We're locked in, we're safe, we're well protected, and I don't want to hear any more about it, you understand? I'm your father and that's final.

DAVID. We all know who you are, Dad.

JOE. *(Points an angry, angry finger.) You,* I'll talk to later... Everybody else, up to bed. I'll turn the lights out.

ROSE. *No!* That's what he's waiting for.

JOE. Then I'll leave them *on.*

ROSE. So he can see better? Are you crazy?

JOE. You want me to call the police?

ROSE. *Not* the police – they steal more than the crooks.

JOE. Then what do you want, Rose? *What do you want?*

ROSE. I want to know that we'll be safe in our beds tonight and that some lunatic isn't going to break into the house and cut our throats and steal my jewels, that's what I want.

SARAH. And the "other thing." We don't want the "other thing" either, Daddy.

DAVID. Why don't we call him in and see if we can negotiate a deal?

JOE. Are you finished? All of you? Because I want to say something... No one is getting into this house tonight. No one is going to cut our throats, steal our jewels or do the "other thing." I guarantee it...but I can't promise it! Because whatever happens, happens. How we live and how we die is in the hands of our maker. We go to sleep and pray we get up in the morning. But if we don't, it's because it's God's will... *God's will,* do you understand? *Do you?*

ROSE. Yes, Joe.

BEN & SARAH. Yes, Daddy.

JOE. Then say it!

ROSE, BEN & SARAH. We understand! It's God's will!

JOE. Thank you! I hope you all feel better... Now, let's go to bed.

DAVID. And pray it ain't "God's will" tonight!

JOE. *(To* **DAVID.***) You* stay! I've postponed that talk we're going to have later to *right now*! Everyone else upstairs.

SARAH. Yes, Daddy... Good night, Daddy.

> *(She kisses him and goes out.)*

BEN. Good night, Dad. And don't worry about anything. I just want you to know that you can count on me.

> *(He goes out.)*

JOE. *(Turns to* **DAVID.***)* You hear? *That's* a son.

DAVID. We all know who he is, Dad.

BEN. *(Calls from the hall.)* Come, Mother.

ROSE. *(To* **JOE.***)* Don't stay down too long, Joe. Come to bed as soon as you're through yelling at David. *(To* **DAVID.***)* Good night, darling. Don't aggravate your father too late.

> *(She leaves,* **JOE** *turns and looks at* **DAVID.***)*

JOE. You want a drink? ...Go ahead!

DAVID. I beg your pardon.

JOE. I said, "Have a drink." This is a special occasion... You and I are going to communicate with each other for the first time in our lives.

DAVID. *(Goes to the bar, picks up a decanter, then puts it down without pouring it.)* I can't do it.

JOE. Why not?

DAVID. It's only fun when you don't like it.

JOE. Ohhh, David! David David David David David David David David David David David David David David David David!

DAVID. Are you talking to me, Dad?

JOE. Yes...but *who* are you? Who *are* you, David? Do you know? Because I don't. I don't know who you are. Do *you* know who you are, David?

DAVID. Just casually. I've seen me around the house.

JOE. *That's* who you are... Quick with a flippant answer. Fresh, disrespectful, unambitious, lazy, no interests, no principles, no beliefs, no scruples, a drunkard, a gambler, a playboy, a lover, a bum, a television watcher and a lousy guitar player, that's who you are.

DAVID. *(Smiles.)* Ah, gee, Dad...you remembered!

JOE. Last week I tried to make a list of all the things you do that make me proud... I didn't even take the top off the fountain pen. In high school, remember the Father and Son Picnic? I went alone. And what makes it so painful to me is that you're the smartest one in the family. You're the smartest one in *anybody's* family. Three college degrees, finished first in your class, and you didn't even show up for your senior year. So why do you throw it all away, David? Why do you drink so much?

DAVID. To overcome this terrible condition I have.

JOE. *(Concerned.)* What condition?

DAVID. Soberness! I get it a lot in the mornings. It's terrible – the room stands still, I can see everything clearly, I get single vision. And then I see the most frightening things in this house... Money, money, money, money, money, money, money, money...

(This breaks **DAVID** *up.)*

JOE. Then why do you stay? Why don't you pack your bottles and leave this house?

DAVID. I have tried on six separate occasions. But it's such a goddamn long driveway, I never could make it to the gate... Sorry about the God reference.

JOE. So you resent all this, is that it? You resent this house, my business, your mother's jewelry, our paintings, the furniture, the swimming pools, is that what you resent?

DAVID. Don't forget our own Baskin-Robbins in the playhouse.

JOE. Your sister likes ice cream – is that a crime? Is it a crime to be rich? Is it a sin to want only the best for your family?

DAVID. I think a man is entitled to whatever he earns in this life. I do, however, think ninety-seven flavors is unnecessary.

JOE. This house could go up in smoke tomorrow, I wouldn't blink an eye. I'll tell you something... There was a time in my life when the holes in my socks were so big, you could put them on from either end... I grew up in a tenement in New York. My mother, my father and eleven kids in one and a half rooms. We had two beds and a cot, you had to take a number off the wall to go to sleep... My father was five foot three, weighed a hundred and twenty-seven pounds. He had a bad heart, bad lungs, bad liver and bad kidneys. He was a piano mover. He died at the age of thirty-two from an acute attack of everything... My mother had to take a job in a sweatshop working six days a week, fourteen hours a day. At night she washed floors at Madison Square Garden, and on Sundays she sold hot sweet potatoes on the corner of Fourteenth Street and Broadway. What she didn't sell was dinner for the rest of the week. Sweet potatoes every night. On Thanksgiving

she'd stuff the sweet potato with a little white potato...
The clothes we wore were made out of rags she found
in the street, or a pair of curtains somebody threw
away... You know what it is for a young boy growing
up in a tough neighborhood in East New York to wear
curtains? Can you picture that? *Fairies* used to beat me
up... And through all those freezing winters and hot,
hungry summers, through all the years of scrimping
and scrubbing, through sicknesses without doctors
or medicines – one winter we all had the whooping
cough at the same time, eleven kids throwing up
simultaneously in one and a half rooms – my mother
nursed us on roller skates...through all that pain and
heartache and suffering, she never complained or cried
out against the world, because she knew it was God's
will. That was the lesson my mother taught us. "What
God has given, God can take away. And for what God
has given you, be thankful." ...When I was fourteen
years old I went to work for the Schreiber Corrugated
Box Company. A rotten man who made a rotten box. No
matter how you packed it, the minute you shipped it, it
fell apart. It didn't hold up under any kind of weather
– including sunshine. Because Schreiber was interested
in a quick profit, not workmanship, not quality. When
I bought the business from him in 1942 with six
thousand dollars my mother saved, I started to make
quality boxes, strong as steel. In the first three months
I lost my mother's six thousand dollars. "It's God's will,"
she kept telling me. And then suddenly business began
to pick up. From nowhere, from *everywhere*, people
were buying my corrugated boxes. It was like a miracle.
The money kept pouring in. I couldn't find banks fast
enough to keep it... My mother never lived to enjoy my
success... On the day I made my first million dollars,
she died peacefully in her sleep on the BMT subway.
Her last words to the conductor were "If God wanted
me to live, I would have taken the bus today." ...All I
wanted for my wife and children was not to suffer the

way I did as a child, not to be deprived of life's barest necessities. But such riches, such wealth? I never asked for it, I never needed it. But when I ask myself, "Why so much? Why all this?" I hear the voice of my mother say, "It's God's will." ...I give half of what I have every year to charity, and the next year I make twice as much. Wealth is as much a responsibility as poverty is a burden. I'll accept whatever is given to me and ask for no more or no less... Can you understand this, David? Does anything I've said to you tonight make any sense at all?

(**DAVID** *snores.*)

He's sleeping! Why do you torture me? Why do you twist my heart around like a pretzel? Where is your faith, David? Have I brought you up without faith, or have you just lost it?

DAVID. If you want, I'll look in my closet in the morning...

JOE. I would give away everything I have in this world if I could just hear you say, "Dear God in heaven, I believe in you."

DAVID. Listen, I'm willing to discuss it with the man... You know his number, call him.

(**DAVID** *gets a whiskey bottle, and heads back to the door.*)

JOE. Oh, David, David. The son who doesn't believe is the father's greatest anguish. Do you know what it says in the Bible, David?

DAVID. Yes, Dad... "This book belongs to the Sheraton-Plaza Hotel." Good night, Dad.

(*He goes out.* **JOE** *stands there, forlorn and defeated. He sighs a mournful sigh. Then he moves to the switch and turns off the lights. The room is in darkness except for the moonlight shining in through the French door. He looks up and speaks softly and reverently.*)

JOE. Am I wrong? ...Is all of this too much for one family? If it is, then why did You give it to me? It's enough already, dear Lord. Don't give me any more... Just David. Give me back my David... If it be Your Will, dear God, that's all I ask... Amen!

> *(A voice, from somewhere in the room itself, is heard.)*

VOICE. Amen!

> *(JOE stops in his tracks, then wheels around.)*

JOE. *(Shocked.) What?* Who's there? Who said that?

VOICE. Don't worry. It's not who you're thinking.

JOE. Who is it? I can't see you.

VOICE. I can't see you either. I lost my glasses. Are the lights on or off?

JOE. You! The one who tried to break in! It's *you*, isn't it?

VOICE. Certainly it's me. Are we inside or outside? I can't see a damn thing.

JOE. Stay where you are! Don't move. I could have the police here in two minutes.

VOICE. You're lucky. In my neighborhood you could wait for them all night... Would you please turn the lights on? I get very nervous in the dark.

JOE. Don't you try anything funny.

VOICE. I'm not here to get laughs.

> *(Suddenly the lights blaze on. JOE is standing with his hand on the switch. He wheels around to face the night visitor.)*

JOE. All right, now who do you –

> *(But there is no one there.)*

Where are you? ...WHERE ARE YOU?

> *(He turns around quickly... Silence. From behind the huge sofa, SIDNEY LIPTON appears on all fours, crawling and feeling the rug with his hands.)*

LIPTON. Don't get excited, I'm just looking for my glasses.

> *(He continues to search. He is not a very impressive-looking person. He wears khaki slacks, a thin raincoat, white sweat socks, Hush Puppies, a tweed cap – a potpourri of cheap clothes.)*

You think the light helps? I still can't see. Where am I, on the floor?

JOE. What do you mean by breaking into my house? Who are you?

LIPTON. *(Still feeling around on the poor.)* Oh, gorgeous rug. This is all handwoven. Must have cost a fortune. What is it, Persian?

JOE. Never mind the rug, I asked you a question. Who are you?

LIPTON. *(Still on his knees.)* The name is Lipton. Sidney Lipton. By the way, were there any calls for me?

JOE. Your wife called.

LIPTON. Sylvia?

JOE. *What do I know your wife's name?*

LIPTON. *(Nods.)* Sylvia. She checks on me every minute. Dreadful woman. If she calls again, I'm not here, all right? ...Where am I, still on the floor?

JOE. *(Takes the glasses out of his pocket.)* Here. Here's your glasses.

LIPTON. You found them? *(Puts out his hand.)* Oh, good. Could you put them in my hand, please?

JOE. Here.

> *(**JOE** puts the glasses into **LIPTON**'s hand.)*

LIPTON. Is that my hand?

JOE. *Certainly* it's your hand.

LIPTON. That'll give you an idea how bad my eyes are. *(He puts the glasses on, still on his knees.)* Ohh. Ohh, yes, there we are... *(Looks up.)* Oh, we're inside, aren't we? *(He looks around.)* Ohhh! *This – this* is gorgeous! *This* is what I call a gorgeous room. This is one of your better showplaces. What is this, the living room?

JOE. Certainly it's the living room... What does it look like?

LIPTON. Do I know? Was I ever invited before? *(Looks around.)* You know what this place reminds me of? *Gatsby...* Did you see *The Great Gatsby*? Wasn't that gorgeous to look at? *Lousy* picture, but beautiful sets –

JOE. Is that why you broke in here? To discuss *movies* with me?

LIPTON. Certainly not. I'm here on business. *Very* important business.

JOE. *What* business?

LIPTON. I'll get to it. Be patient. Let me look around. *(Admiringly caresses the carved facade of the fireplace.)* How often does a person like me get inside one of these big-time houses? ...Do you have something soft to drink? R.C. Cola? A Yoo-hoo?

JOE. If you have business with me, you make an appointment like everyone else.

LIPTON. *(Looking around.)* My business is not the kind of business you think, and I'm not like everyone else. *(Points to an ornate armchair.)* I love the chair. I don't fall in love easily, but I am in love with this chair. Just for curiosity, what did you pay? Three thousand? Thirty-four hundred? Am I being pushy?

JOE. I don't remember what I paid for chairs. Is that what you are? An antique dealer?

LIPTON. Antiques? No. Antiquity, perhaps.

JOE. What does that mean?

LIPTON. What does *anything* mean?

JOE. What do you mean by "What does *anything* mean"?

LIPTON. What is meant by meaning? What is the meaning of "meant"? What is real or unreal? What is here, what is there? What the hell are we talking about? I don't know – I'm still dizzy from that fall I took.

JOE. I can't make you out. You're not a burglar, that I can tell.

LIPTON. A burglar? No. An antique dealer? No. But who am I? What am I? Why am I here? That's the mystery, isn't it? God, I love a good mystery. Did you see *Chinatown*? Jack Nicholson, Faye Dunaway? They cut his nose, he wore a bandaid for two hours. Three-fifty a ticket to see a man with a slit nose, where do they get the nerve? A nice picture, but I can see slit noses for free at Mount Sinai –

JOE. If you don't tell me who you are, it's not your *nose* that's going to get slit.

LIPTON. Ah, ah, you're losing patience, aren't you? Mustn't lose patience. All in good time. Patience, Joe, patience. *(Looks at a crystal vase.)* Lovely crystal. Who picked it out, your wife, Rose?

JOE. How do you know my wife, Rose?

LIPTON. Did I say I knew her?

JOE. But you mentioned her name.

LIPTON. To mention her name is not to say I know her. Ergo, to know is to meet... Ergo, to be is not necessarily to exist... Ergo, to know is to question, to question is to ask... Ergo, what is meant by knowing and what is meant by "ergo"? ...Oh, God, I have such pains in the head. I could use an aspirin, Valium, acupuncture, anything.

JOE. You're not getting anything from me until I get some information from *you*!

LIPTON. Interesting. You're not as tall as I expected. They led me to believe you were a bigger man – six four, six five. Not that it matters... You know how tall Alan Ladd was?

JOE. I'M NOT INTERESTED IN ALAN LADD!

LIPTON. Two inches shorter than Veronica Lake. They never made a movie where they had a child... They couldn't find one small enough. I *love* movie gossip...

JOE. Who's been talking to you? What do you know about me?

LIPTON. I know a lot and I know nothing! Yet to know nothing is to know everything... Why do I say things like that? What does that mean? I have cramps in the head. Did you ever get cramps in the head?

JOE. A lunatic! A lunatic wandered into my house from the snow. Why do I answer you? Why do I bother talking to you?

LIPTON. Curiosity! There is something curious about me, you've got to admit... All right, enough chitchat, enough fiddle-faddle, enough fencing with each other. Let's get down to brass tacks, Joe Benjamin. Let's discuss the reason of the mysterious midnight visit of this most curious and somewhat sinister figure standing in front of you. Why, at this hour, on this night, in this year, in this city, in this house, on this rug, in these shoes, do I, Sidney Leonard Lipton stand before you? WHAT BUSINESS DO WE, STRANGERS TILL NOT FIVE MINUTES AGO, HAVE UNTO EACH OTHER?

JOE. Are you selling something? If you're a salesman I'll kill you with my bare hands!

LIPTON. Do I look like a salesman? Do I look like a man who deals in goods and hardware? I am a man of flair, of fancy, a bizarre and unique guide to the world beyond our world, a companion into wild and soaring flights beyond human comprehension.

JOE. A travel agent? Is that what you are, a travel agent?

LIPTON. *(Yells, angrily.) You have no imagination!* I am trying to jazz this up. I have a wonderful sense of the theatrical, and you keep pulling my curtain down. What do I have to do to tell you who I am? Think, Joe, think!

JOE. I think you're a *nut,* that's what I think, and I want you out! *(He grabs **LIPTON** by the arm.)* Out, do you hear me? OUT!

LIPTON. Easy, easy. No rough stuff, I'm not a physical person.

JOE. Ten seconds and I throw you out that window head-first. One, two –

LIPTON. Don't force my hand. I deal a heavy hand –

JOE. Three, four –

LIPTON. *(Stops; points a long finger.) STAY! I STAY YOU!* Yea, you would banish He who brings thee the gift of life and the eternal bliss of the joyful soul? ...Forget that! Forget I said that. That was a slip. A boo-boo. Slipsies! I have a charley horse in the middle of my temple. Does Ben-Gay work on the head?

JOE. I'm getting a funny feeling. There's something funny going on here. You're not who you pretend to be at all, are you?

LIPTON. Aha! Aha, getting somewhere. Getting warm...

JOE. This is all an act. A game. Something is up, here... Somebody sent you, didn't they?

LIPTON. Hot! Getting hot!

JOE. Somebody sent you to get something from me!

LIPTON. Hotter! Hotter! Boiling hotter!

JOE. Somebody important who knows me sent you to get something that I have that has enormous value.

LIPTON. Boiling! Roasting, burning, boiling! August fifteenth through the twentieth – scorching.

JOE. Something I have that no other man on earth has.

LIPTON. *Scalding! Steaming lava!* Two weeks in a sauna bath!

JOE. My Bible! My Gutenberg Bible!

LIPTON. Cold. Freezing cold. Winter. A room for two in Toronto.

JOE. Damn you, what is it?

> *(He bangs his fist on the table.)*

LIPTON. Hey! Hey hey hey! Calm! Calm, please. Take it easy. Let's not break our blood vessels. Let's behave

ourselves. The last thing I want is for you to get sick.
I mean, you *are* in good health, aren't you?

JOE. *(Knocks wood.)* Thank God!

LIPTON. *Hot! Boiling hot! Getting hot again!*

JOE. What? Good health?

LIPTON. Cold.

JOE. Knocking on wood?

LIPTON. Cold, cold...

JOE. Thank God?

LIPTON. HOT! HOT AS A PISTOL! THE FOURTH OF
JULY! AN ALL-TIME RECORD BREAKER!

JOE. *(Screams.)* What are you saying? You're driving me
crazy with these stupid games.

LIPTON. Temper, temper. What a nervous disposition. And
I was told you were such a patient, wonderful man.

JOE. Who told you? Who told you I was a wonderful man?

LIPTON. *(Softly; side of his mouth.)* You know.

JOE. I *don't* know.

LIPTON. *(Softly again.)* Sure, you do, Joe... *He* did.

JOE. Who's he?

LIPTON. He! Him! Capital "H," small "i" small "m" ...Do
I have to spell it out for you? Oh, I just did, didn't I?
Went on and on about you. Crazy about you. I'll tell you
the truth, you're His favorite. Out of everyone. I don't
mean just this neighborhood, I mean EVERYONE!
Yes, you, Joe Benjamin, are considered to be His –
that's capital "H" again – His absolute favorite. And
that is the honest to God's truth... God's truth...

> *(He makes a cross on his chest, then a circle, a
> square, all sorts of signs – then unbuttons his
> raincoat, revealing a football jersey with an
> enormous letter "G" on the front.)*

Am I getting through to you at all?

JOE. I can't understand what you're saying.

LIPTON. *Can't* understand or *afraid* to understand?

JOE. Afraid? I'm not afraid of anything on the face of this earth except God himself.

LIPTON. BINGO! BULL'S-EYE! Ding-a-ling-a-ling-a-ling! Fire, fire, fire! Home run, home run!

(He jumps around in an excited jig.)

JOE. STOP IT! I beg of you to stop it and tell me who you are, in plain, simple language. I'm a plain, simple man, I can't understand all this fancy hocus-pocus rigmarole. Who are you, please?

*(**LIPTON** stands erect, clasps his fingers together.)*

LIPTON. *(Solemnly.)* Very well. Forgive me, my son. I have taken these extraordinary measures, this bizarre form, so that I might present myself to you in some acceptable dimension, for had I told you the truth straight on of my identity, even *I* could not have given you the power to accept or comprehend. Yes, Joe – I am – who you think I am!

JOE. *(Sits on the sofa.)* Are you trying to tell me that you're – that you're – are you trying to tell me –

LIPTON. Say it, Joe. You will only believe if you say the words yourself.

JOE. – that you – are you trying to say that you – ?

LIPTON. Yes, yes… I can't answer unless you ask me, Joe.

JOE. I can't get the words out. It's so *inconceivable* to me.

LIPTON. Conceive it, Joe. Get the words out. *Who*, Joe? Who am I trying to tell you who I am?

JOE. *God?* Are you trying to tell me that you're *God?*

LIPTON. Who? …God? GOD? Is *that* what you thought? That I was going to say I was God? My God, that I never figured on. Nothing personal, but that's really crazy. Why? Do I look like God? Would God wear a filthy Robert Hall raincoat and a pair of leaky Hush Puppies? In the winter? Would God wear glasses? I mean, if anyone's going to have good eyes, it's going to be God. He's the one who gave them out... No, Joe, I'm sorry to disappoint you, but I am not God.

(He sits on the sofa.)

JOE. Then who are you?

LIPTON. I'm a friend of God's.

JOE. (His body sags.) I can't take any more of this.

LIPTON. Not a *close* friend. We met a few times.

JOE. You met God?

LIPTON. Twice on business, once on a boat ride.

JOE. What business? *What business do you have with God?*

LIPTON. My capacity is such that I perform services for Him that deal with vital and important functions in areas related to the contact of individuals whose special interests –

JOE. *What business?*

LIPTON. *I deliver messages!*

JOE. You're a messenger boy?

LIPTON. (Hurt, indignant.) Don't say it like that. I'm not a lousy kid from Western Union, I work for God!

JOE. You're a messenger from God?

LIPTON. Important documents only; no packages.

JOE. I don't believe you.

LIPTON. Nobody does. Not even Sylvia. She laughs when I tell her... What am I going to do, bring my boss home for dinner?

JOE. You're either drunk, a madman or both.

LIPTON. Don't start in, please, I have a headache that goes right into my hat. Even my eyeglasses throb. Didn't I tell you you wouldn't believe me? Look, Mr. Benjamin, I understand you're a wonderful man. Charitable, philanthropic, religious. Am I right?

JOE. I serve God as best I can.

LIPTON. So if He can have servants, why can't He afford messengers? He's got cleaning people, I've seen them.

JOE. All right, if you're who you say you are –

LIPTON. I am.

JOE. Let me finish!

LIPTON. When you finish, I am!

JOE. *If you're who you say you are* – a messenger of God – then where do you come from?

LIPTON. Oh, you mean like heaven? The Eternal Paradise? Where the angels abide? A place like that?

JOE. Yes.

LIPTON. Jackson Heights. It's in Queens, just over the Triborough Bridge. Look, I'm not *Here Comes Mr. Jordan.* I'm a nine-to-fiver. This is strictly a job with me. I was sent by an agency, I was interviewed, I had to have a bicycle – it was stolen from me in Central Park. I told them we should work in pairs.

JOE. But you said you met God.

LIPTON. Not face-to-face. There's always a big light over Him – the glare is murder.

JOE. But you've been in His presence.

LIPTON. We're *all* in His presence.

JOE. But *have you seen Him*? Actually seen him with your own eyes?

LIPTON. Without my glasses, I wouldn't recognize my own wife.

JOE. *With* your glasses.

LIPTON. *With* my glasses? Yes, I'd recognize her.

JOE. GOD! GOD! HAVE YOU SEEN GOD?

LIPTON. I didn't actually *see* Him. I heard Him.

JOE. He spoke to you?

LIPTON. He blessed me.

JOE. God blessed you?

LIPTON. I sneezed and God blessed me – what do you want from me?

JOE. This isn't a practical joke, is it? Did David hire you? My son David put you up to this, didn't he? I wouldn't put it past him.

LIPTON. I have not had the pleasure of meeting the boy, but personally he sounds like a lot of trouble... Can we get on with this, please? I have a migraine starting in my hair.

JOE. Get on with *what*? With this *insanity*?

LIPTON. *(Loudly.)* I cannot deliver God's message until you accept that I am God's messenger! What do I need to prove it to you, *wings*? ...I should have flapped in here like a Perdue chicken, then you would have believed me, wouldn't you?

JOE. Tell me *why*? Then maybe I'll believe you. *Why* would God send a message to me, Joe Benjamin, a plain, simple, ordinary man?

LIPTON. *To test your faith, that's why!* ...Strike that! I didn't say that! You didn't hear it! Erase! Eighty-six on the first sentence! I'm not supposed to tell you that... Do you have any uppers? Ask David, I bet he's got pills.

JOE. Test my faith? *My* faith? My lifeblood is my faith! Are you saying that God doesn't believe my faith in Him?

LIPTON. Oh, no. Not Him. *He* believes! God's crazy about you... It's the other one.

JOE. What other one?

LIPTON. *(Softly, slyly.)* You know...the *other* one. From downstairs... Mr. Nasty... Bad, Bad Leroy Brown... Oh, for God's sakes, you have to spell out *everything* for you... Satan! Lucifer! The *Devil*, all right? ...I can't believe this conversation. I feel like I'm on *Sesame Street*.

JOE. *(Smiles.)* The *Devil*? The *Devil* questions my faith in God? *(He laughs.)* Are you going to tell me now you met the Devil?

LIPTON. Who do you think stole my bicycle? ...Would you like to know what the Devil looks like? Robert Redford, I swear on my mother's grave. Gorgeous. The man is gorgeous. Blond hair, little bend in the nose –

JOE. *(Moving toward the phone.)* I've wasted enough time with you, I'm calling the police!

LIPTON. *(Points a long arm and finger again.)* Stay! I stay you! I render you powerless and motionless!

*(**JOE** picks up the phone and dials.)*

All right, I can't do it, but put down the phone, please. I'll tell you everything,

*(**JOE** looks at him, puts down the receiver.)*

I'll tell you what I know, take it or leave it... God and Satan were sitting around having one of those boring philosophical debates – this was a week ago Tuesday. And Satan was sitting there in this pink suit – gorgeous tan, little mole on his cheek... And Satan says there is not one man on the face of the earth, in the entire universe – regardless of race, religion, Polish, whatever – who would not renounce God once the Devil put enough heat on. Can you believe it? Two grown deities talking like this? To which *God* said – this is a quote, they got it on tape – *one* man would never renounce. And that man is... *(Makes a bugle sound.)* Ta tum ta tum ta tum ta tum ta taaa... JOE BENJAMIN! Thrills, right? ...So they make a bet – I'm only telling you what I heard – and the bet is, the Devil will make your life so miserable, you'll renounce God! So-o-o, that's it. Hell of a story, isn't it?

JOE. Renounce God? You think I would renounce God?

LIPTON. Tonight, no. When they shut off your steam, who knows?

JOE. You think so little of man that he would renounce *God* in the face of adversity?

LIPTON. I've seen people with a burning engine on a 747 who would sell out God in a second for a little good news from the pilot... So you believe me – good. I can deliver my message and run. *(Takes out a folded, dirty scrap of paper.)* You ready?

JOE. Let me see that.

LIPTON. *(Pulls it away.)* I have to read it. It's not official unless I read it...

(He takes a pillow from the sofa, throws it on the floor, and indicates that **JOE** *should kneel on it.* **JOE** *looks around hesitantly,* **LIPTON** *nods that it's all right,* **JOE** *reluctantly gets on his knees, feeling foolish and embarrassed.)*

Here we go. "Joseph Marvin Benjamin..."

JOE. Melvin.

LIPTON. What?

JOE. Joseph *Melvin* Benjamin.

LIPTON. *(Squints at the paper.)* Melvin – right. Would you believe God has such a lousy handwriting? ... "Joseph Melvin Benjamin of 118 Park Place Drive, Oyster Bay, Long Island, zip 11771 – "

JOE. Come on, come on, get on with it.

LIPTON. "Husband of Rose, father of David, Ben and Sarah, son of Arnold and Jeanette – "

JOE. Get to the *message* already!

LIPTON. "To Joseph Melvin Benjamin, devoted husband and father...if you cherish your children and wife, the house that shelters you, the clothes that warm you and the flesh that covers you, if pain, calamity and disaster do not in any manner whatsoever appeal to you, then renounce your God!" That's it! Message delivered. No tip necessary, it's taken care of. Good night, good luck, God bless you...but I doubt it!

(He puts the message back in his pocket and starts for the French door.)

JOE. Wait a minute! Where are you going?

LIPTON. If I had a choice, Fort Lauderdale... Unfortunately, the bus stop!

(He turns and starts out again.)

JOE. It doesn't make sense. Why? Why should I, a man who has believed in God all his life, suddenly renounce Him?

LIPTON. I take home a hundred-thirty-seven dollars a week. If you want theological advice call Billy Graham. Can I get the number fifteen bus on this corner?

JOE. I will *not* renounce God. I will *never* renounce God, do you hear me?

LIPTON. Renounce, don't renounce, what do I care? ...I have to walk out in the freezing snow wearing Supphose.

JOE. I am the servant of God, He is my Maker. I fear Him and love Him but come hell or high water, I will never renounce Him!

LIPTON. Can I be honest? You can count on the hell and high water. Good luck, Joe. I know you've got what it takes. And no matter what terrible things happen to you, remember that God loves you!

JOE. And I love Him!

LIPTON. But in case the romance falls apart, here's my number. Renouncements are toll-free calls.

> *(We hear a fire engine clanging in the distance.)*

JOE. What's that?

LIPTON. I don't know.

JOE. What's going on out there?

LIPTON. *(Looks out the window.)* Looks like a fire. Near the water... Where's your factory?

JOE. Near the water.

LIPTON. Ohh... Look at that burn. Like a cardboard box... What do you make?

JOE. Cardboard boxes.

LIPTON. Ohh... Well, I wouldn't worry unless I got a phone call.

> *(The phone rings. They both look at it.)*

JOE. It's not my plant. My plant is a hundred percent fireproof.

> *(**JOE** picks up the phone.)*

JOE. Hello? ...Eddie? ...What is it? ...What? ...*What?*

LIPTON. One more "what" and you're in trouble.

JOE. *(Into the phone.)* WHAT?

LIPTON. What is it, a disaster or a calamity?

JOE. *(Into the phone.)* The *whole plant*?

LIPTON. Oh, a catastrophe, wonderful!

JOE. Thank you, Eddie... I know it wasn't your fault.

> *(He hangs up.)*

LIPTON. How much did the insurance cover?

JOE. *(Dazed.)* I didn't have insurance. I didn't believe in insurance... GOD was my insurance.

LIPTON. Really? Well, that was your mistake. Even God is with John Hancock... So long, Joe.

> *(And he is gone.)*

> *(Curtain.)*

Scene Two

(The scene is the Benjamin living room, two weeks later, at dinner time. It is dark outside. Some of the furniture has been removed, and some of the paintings. A fruit box replaces a chair. We can hear the bitter cold winter wind howling through the trees. The house seems bleak.)

(The telephone rings... And again. The oak door leading from the dining room opens, and MORRIS *enters. He is wearing his white serving jacket and black tie, but on top of this he has on his heavy winter overcoat, gloves, a muffler and earmuffs. It is obviously freezing in the house. He carries a silver tray from which he has just served food.)*

(As he crosses to the phone, the family shouts in from the dining room, "Morris, close the door," "It's freezing," etc. A hand from inside slams the dining room door shut. The phone continues to ring, MORRIS *answers it.)*

MORRIS. Hello. Benjamin residence... Who's calling, please? ...Mr. Benjamin's having a cold dinner with his family just now... Yes, sir... One moment, sir.

(He puts the receiver down and crosses toward the dining room, blowing on his hands, doing a little dance to keep warm. He opens the door and calls in.)

Mr. Benjamin?

JOE. Yes?

MORRIS. It's a Mr. Lipton.

JOE. *(Offstage.)* Who?

MORRIS. Mr. Sidney Lipton. He wants to know if you'd like it a little colder in the house. Then he giggled.

JOE. *(Offstage.)* Wait a minute, I'm coming.

> (**JOE** *comes out of the dining room. He wears a full-length man's fur coat, a beaver hat and gloves. He leaves the door open, and they all yell in from the dining room, "Close the door," "Its freezing," etc.)*

JOE. Morris, close the door. And sit on my chair – keep it warm.

MORRIS. Yes, sir.

> *(He goes into the dining room and closes the door,* **JOE** *picks up the phone.)*

JOE. *(Into the phone.)* What do you want? ...I told you last night and the night before and I'll tell you every night you call me, I'm not renouncing anything, you understand? I don't care how cold it gets in here. I'll burn all the furniture before I say yes to you... And don't bother calling me any more...because they're cutting off my phone tomorrow.

> *(He hangs up the phone angrily. The dining room door opens again, and* **ROSE** *and* **SARAH** *come out.* **SARAH** *wears a ski suit;* **ROSE** *has on a fur coat, boots and a mink hat.)*

ROSE. My hands are frozen, Joe. Morris had to cut the meat for me.

SARAH. *(Holds her teeth.)* My teeth are numb.

> (**BEN** *enters wearing a ski suit just like* **SARAH**'s.)

BEN. Oh, my sinuses. My sinuses, Mother. They're frozen solid.

> (**DAVID** *enters wearing a wool jacket and motorcycle helmet.)*

DAVID. Attention, everybody! I have good news and bad news.

SARAH. *(Hopefully.)* What's the good news?

DAVID. The heat is back on.

BEN. What's the bad news?

DAVID. I lied.

BEN. I hate him! I hate him, Mother!

> *(The lights dim, then blink up again.)*

ROSE. What's going on? Why is everything suddenly falling apart? No water, no heat, the electricity is almost gone. What's happening to us?

DAVID. *(A big smile.)* It's just like living in the city.

> *(They all chime in with questions – "Yeah, what's going on?," etc.)*

JOE. Can I have a little decorum? A little decorum, everybody. Please! Mady! Morris!

> *(**MADY** and **MORRIS** enter, shivering.)*

Will you all sit down, please? What I have to say to you all now is of grave importance... You may have heard it said before, to love God is not to question God. We must accept God as we accept the air and the sky, the earth and the sun.

ROSE. Will this take long, Joe? My eyelashes are caking up from the frost.

JOE. None of us are very comfortable, Rose. None of us like living under these conditions. We've had it very good for a long time. We're just going to have to learn to live more economically, tighten our belts –

MADY. I can't cut the meat thinner unless you want me to shave it.

JOE. I understand, Mady... There is, however, one thing I haven't had the courage to tell you until tonight... My dear children, devoted wife, faithful servants... Have any of you stopped to think why, after a lifetime of luxury and prosperity, we're suddenly living in a house that's twelve degrees colder than it is outside? Have you wondered why plumbers, electricians, supermarkets have all turned their backs on us? Why a butcher that

I have personally kept in business for fifteen years, by buying the finest beef in the world, sends over meat that three of our cats walked away from? The answer is... These things are happening because they are *meant* to happen. The truth is... I am being tested! Tested for my courage and strength.

(There is a moment's silence as they all look at him, puzzled.)

ROSE. Is this for an insurance policy, Joe?

JOE. *(Looks heavenward.)* How do I explain this? Look... I'm fifty-six years old. And in all that time, besides my love for all of you, I've believed in only one thing... The Divine Wisdom and Glory of God.

MADY. Aaaaa-men! Right on!

JOE. Thank you, Mady. Now, God, in His infinite wisdom, has seen fit to give us all the fruits of this earth... But now, still in His infinite wisdom, He has seen fit to take it away from us... Two weeks ago, I had an experience... with a man...

ROSE. Oh, God! Do you want the children to hear this, Joe?

JOE. *(Irritated.)* Let me finish! ...Don't ask me who he was or where he came from. Just accept what I tell you... It is my belief, that I have been chosen, for reasons unknown to me, out of all the people on the face of the earth – regardless of race, religion, Polish whatever – to test the faith and courage of man in his love and devotion to God.

(There is a long silence. They all look at each other.)

ROSE. Is this something that came in the mail, Joe?

JOE. It didn't come in the mail.

BEN. What do you mean a test, Dad? You have to cut out meats and fish, is that what you mean?

JOE. Why doesn't anybody listen to me? Don't you understand? God is asking me to make the supreme personal sacrifice.

ROSE. Wait a minute, Joe... Does that mean we have to take
two of those Jehovah's Witnesses from Ohio in to live
with us?

JOE. You know what I think? I think *this family* is part
of my test. And I'm not so sure I can pass. *(To* DAVID.*)*
I never thought I would be turning to you for help.
You're a bum, but you're smart. Do *you* understand
me?

DAVID. Yes, Dad. I think so.

JOE. Thank you. Will *you* please explain it to them?

DAVID. I'm not certain about this, but I think Dad's going
into a convent.

(BEN *and* SARAH *giggle,* DAVID *is hysterical.)*

JOE. *(Glares at him.)* You know what I pray for? I pray
I had my money back again so I could cut you off
without a cent. *(He paces; angrily.)* All right, listen to
me, everybody. I will try and make this as simple as
possible. Two weeks ago a man broke into this house.
The one whose glasses we found. His name was Sidney
Lipton – a weirdo. A nut, lunatic weirdo. He wore Hush
Puppies and talked about Alan Ladd, *Chinatown* with
Jack Nicholson and Veronica Lake –

ROSE. Veronica Lake wasn't in *Chinatown.*

JOE. *(He bites his hat.)* Don't analyze it, Rose. Just listen...
Lipton was not who he pretended to be. He played the
fool because he knew I would never accept his real
identity until he proved it to me... Well, he proved it, all
right. Oh, brother, did he prove it.

BEN. Are you going to tell us, Dad?

JOE. Very well... Sidney Lipton, the man who appeared
before me, was a messenger – of God!

(A long silence.)

ROSE. *(To* MADY.*) Who* did he say?

JOE. For *God!* *God!* He delivers messages for *God!*

SARAH. For *God,* Daddy?

ROSE. *Our* God, Joe?

JOE. Yes! YES!

ROSE. Joe, don't get upset... We all know what a strain you're under, getting wiped out and all... Think, sweetheart, are you sure he wasn't from UNICEF?

JOE. HE-WAS-FROM-GOD! God sent him to talk to me.

ROSE. What was it like, Joe? Did you hear organ music? Could you see through him?

JOE. He's not what you think. He's a regular person. Like you or me. It's just a job. They hired him. He lives in Jackson Heights. He takes home a hundred and thirty-seven dollars a week. They stole his bicycle. He wants to move to Fort Lauderdale.

ROSE. He won't like it there. It's all little condominiums now.

> (**JOE** *bangs the floor with his fist in frustration. The family goes into a huddle, then they turn, all smiles.*)

BEN. Dad, you never lied to us in your life. If you saw him, then I believe you. We all do.

JOE. Thank you. Thank you, all of you.

DAVID. May I ask one question?

MADY. Uh-oh.

DAVID. Am I to understand that some fruitcake from Queens walks in here and tells you he's a messenger from God?

JOE. Important documents only. No packages.

DAVID. I see... And what was he like. How did he strike you as a person?

JOE. He got cramps in his head...

DAVID. Figures... And how did you know he was a messenger from God? Did he have identification?

JOE. Yes.

DAVID. What was it?

JOE. He had a big "G" on his sweatshirt.

DAVID. A big "G"! Are you sure he wasn't from Georgia Tech?

JOE. You must believe me. He was God's messenger.

DAVID. And what was the message?

JOE. The message was... I should renounce God.

SARAH. Renounce God?

ROSE. Joe, that's terrible. Are you sure he had the right address?

JOE. There's no mistake. That was the message.

BEN. Who asked you this, Dad? Who wants you to renounce God?

JOE. God does. God asked me. To prove to the Devil how much I love God.

DAVID. Ah, the Devil's in on it too... Big "D" on the sweatshirt, Dad?

JOE. I didn't see him. The messenger did.

DAVID. The messenger saw the Devil? ... *(Big smile.)* And what did he look like?

JOE. You'll never believe it.

ROSE. Tell us, Joe. We'll believe it.

JOE. The good-looking one. From *Butch Cassidy.*

ROSE. Paul Newman?

JOE. No. The other one.

ROSE. Robert Redford? He's such a clean-cut looking boy.

JOE. You don't understand anything. He loves me.

ROSE. Robert Redford?

JOE. No! God loves me.

ROSE. We all love you, Joe. But we wouldn't ask you to renounce us. That's why I'm very surprised at God.

JOE. Listen to me. He not only loves me, I happen to be His favorite. The messenger told me.

SARAH. God's favorite? Oh, Daddy, how wonderful.

BEN. *(Very serious.)* That's a great honor, Dad. Congratulations.

JOE. Can I finish, please? It's God's belief that no matter how much pain and hardship I suffer, I will never renounce Him. So He's putting me to this test. That's why the business burned down, why we have no heat, no water... Don't you see how wonderful it is? I've been chosen out of all the people on earth to prove to God Himself how much I love Him.

ROSE. Ohhhhhh! Ohhhhhh, I see... We all have to suffer because God loves you so much. Oh, Joe, I'm so proud of you. You must be thrilled to death.

BEN. Nice going, Dad.

SARAH. I can't wait to tell my friends.

MADY. Wait'll the girls on the bus hear this.

ALL. That's wonderful! etc.

MADY. Mr. Benjamin! Mr. Benjamin!

(They hug each other.)

DAVID. *(Starts to laugh, then gets hysterical.)* I love it! I love it! *(He is beside himself with joy.)* A nut with a big "G" on his sweatshirt walks in here and says he's a messenger of God and you all believe it! I love it, I love it, I LOVE IT!

(He crosses to near the French door.)

JOE. He doesn't believe it. *(To **DAVID**.)* The fire in the factory was *real*, wasn't it? The freezing cold in here is real – and it's just the beginning. The *real* test begins tonight. He just told me on the phone. What we have to face in these next two weeks, don't even try to imagine.

ROSE. I can just imagine!

BEN. Dad, you know you can count on me.

JOE. Thank you, son.

SARAH. Me too, Dad.

ROSE. *(Goes over to **MADY**.)* Just like her twin brother. They were always so close, even as children, weren't they, Mady?

MADY. I *still* can't tell them apart.

DAVID. Is it my turn to vote? I registered, you know.

(*They all turn and look at* **DAVID**.)

JOE. Yes, David, it's your turn now.

DAVID. My personal opinion? We've got a terrific lawsuit on our hands... I say we should sue God for property damage.

JOE. Don't get smart! You don't know what you're dealing with.

DAVID. Are you trying to tell me that God has decided to test man's faith in Him by sending this family a tough cut of pot roast?

JOE. Be careful, David, I'm begging you.

DAVID. Well, at least let's stand up and fight Him! I mean, the Man's been pushing people around for twenty-five thousand years. I don't think we have to take *any more crap from Him.*

ROSE. Oh, my God!

SARAH. Wow!

BEN. Oh, brother!

MADY. If we wasn't in trouble before, we are in trouble *now!*

JOE. Don't you talk like that in this house, do you hear me? *I will not have that kind of language in this house!*

DAVID. Then how about *outside* the house?

(*He quickly opens the French door, goes out on the portico and yells up to the heavens.*)

Hey, God, You want to test us? Here we are! You want us to show You what we're made of? Show us what *You're* made of! ...What about it, Big Fella, *show us a little muscle!*

(*He starts to laugh with glee, and at that very moment, an enormous clap of thunder erupts and a bolt of lightning hits the portico, just missing* **DAVID** *and leaving a ball of smoke. The drapes fall down, and books tumble off*)

their shelves. The women scream and **DAVID**
rushes back into the room, ashen white.)

Ho-ly *shit*!

*(There is another clap of thunder and another
bolt of lightning on the portico. The women
scream again.)*

JOE. *(To* **DAVID**.*) Now* see what you've done!

MORRIS. *(To* **DAVID**.*)* Mr. David, I never told you this before,
but *you've got a big mouth*!

*(Another clap of thunder and another bolt of
lightning; more smoke.)*

JOE. In the basement, everybody! Quick, Morris, get
everyone down into the basement.

*(***MORRIS** *starts to usher everyone out of the
room as the thunder and lightning keep
coming.)*

MORRIS. Come on, everyone, follow me!

DAVID. Me first! Me first!

(He's the first one out.)

ROSE. Joe, don't stand there, you'll be killed!

JOE. Go on, Rose, go with the children... I'll be right down,
I promise.

ROSE. If you get a chance, get my bracelets.

(And she is gone. They are all gone except **JOE**.
*There is one final clap of thunder and one
final bolt of lightning as* **JOE** *gets on his knees
and prays.)*

JOE. Forgive him, dear God. Forgive my son, David. It's
not *his* fault. Let *me* pay for his sins, Lord. Help me to
teach him. Help me... Help me...

*(There is another bolt of lightning and a
crack of thunder. And suddenly* **SIDNEY
LIPTON** *rushes in through the French door, his*

*raincoat smoldering and smoking. He slaps
at it, trying to put himself out.)*

LIPTON. What about helping *me*? Water! Water! Throw
water on me, I'm smoking! Hot! Hot! Burning hot!
...My good raincoat, for Christ's sakes! I needed it
dry-cleaned, not toasted!

*(He gets a seltzer bottle from the bar and
sprays his coat.)*

JOE. What are *you* doing here?

LIPTON. You got a crazy son, you know that? I could have
been killed! *Never* get God angry when a person is
standing under a tree.

JOE. I'm sorry. I apologize for David.

LIPTON. It's a little late, isn't it? God heard what he said. I'd
hate to be driving on the Long Island Expressway with
that kid... Am I out? Am I still smoldering?

JOE. You mustn't pay attention to what David said. He's
young, he's angry at the world, at all the injustices he
sees... He doesn't understand the ways of God.

LIPTON. "Crap." He actually said the word "crap" to God.
I couldn't believe it. I mean, it's bad enough to fool
around with Mother Nature.

*(He goes over to the phone and starts to dial.
He dials about thirty digits...)*

JOE. Who are you calling?

LIPTON. What?

JOE. Who are you calling?

LIPTON. *(Points heavenward; into the phone.)* Hello... Is He
in? ...Who's this? ...Oh, His service... No, don't wake
Him... I'll call back later.

(He hangs up.)

JOE. If you could just explain to God. He's just a boy. I'll do
anything. Give you whatever I have...

LIPTON. Hey! Hey! What's this – a bribe? Are you offering
me a bribe? Are you trying to bribe *me*, a messenger of
God?

JOE. No! No, of course not!

LIPTON. Why not? Too good for you? I'll take anything – cash, clothes, canned goods, sheets, linens – whatever you got. I took *some* beating on the market this week.

JOE. I'm sorry.

LIPTON. *You're* sorry? You still got a gorgeous roof over your head. I just got a twelve percent rent increase. And they took out the elevator. Six-floor walk-up and Sylvia just got her report back from the doctors... Positive varicose veins. If I don't get her out of New York this winter, they'll have to tie her ankles in knots. SO DON'T TELL ME YOUR TROUBLES WITH YOUR LOUSY SON!

(He sits, and opens up his attaché case.)

JOE. I'm sorry. Sometimes you get so involved with your own problems, you forget about others.

LIPTON. People don't care about people any more. Well, you're finding that out, aren't you? I can't hear myself. *(He rubber-stamps papers.)* I think the thunder deviated my septum... Well, on with business. *(Takes out papers from his briefcase.)* If I can just have your signature, I'll be able to get home in time for the *Hollywood Squares. (Hands a pen to* **JOE**.*)* Sign all three copies – write, don't print.

JOE. Sign what? *(Looks at the papers.)* What is this for?

LIPTON. For the ad.

JOE. What ad?

LIPTON. The ad in *The New York Times.*

JOE. What ad? What *New York Times*? What the hell are you talking about?

LIPTON. Language, language, please. I can't take any more thunder. I'm sure you and your family have suffered enough too. You don't have to take this any more... So we'd like you to take a small ad in the Sunday *Times* saying you've renounced God... We pay for it – we get a rate.

JOE. Are you mad?

LIPTON. At you, no. At your son, a little. Sign here, your full name in triplicate.

JOE. Get away! I'm not signing any documents.

LIPTON. It's not a document. It's a lousy piece of paper. The Magna Carta was a document. Don't make such a big deal –

JOE. Get away! *(He grabs the papers and throws them in the air.)* Get away, I said!

LIPTON. *(Starts to pick up the scattered papers.)* Keep it up! Keep that up and you're going to bring on humidity like you've never seen in your life. You'll have to go to a garage to get your underwear off. *(He has retrieved the papers.)* Don't you understand? It's not an official renouncement unless it appears in the Sunday *New York Times*... The *Daily News* is acceptable only in the Bronx and Staten Island.

JOE. *I am not taking an ad renouncing God!*

LIPTON. It's a small ad – tiny little type like "Doggies Lost." Who's even going to see it? The printer and a few nuts who look for renouncements.

JOE. Never! Never never never never never never!

LIPTON. Joe, you're a businessman. When you go bankrupt, it's not legal unless it's in the paper, right? ...We'll put it under "Montauk Fishing News" – who the hell reads that?

JOE. Didn't you just hear "Never never never never never never"?

LIPTON. I heard, I wasn't sure it was definite... Here, take the pen.

JOE. Get that *poisonous* thing away from me!

LIPTON. *(Looks at it.)* Poisonous? A Bic Banana? ...Joe, listen to me. You don't know these people... You don't know what discomfort they're capable of. I'm talking about the big-time pain... In exactly one minute you're going to start to itch. There is *no* itch which itches like the itch you're going to get, Joe. There is not enough Johnson's baby powder in the world that could help you... Sign, Joe!

JOE. You think I don't know what hardship is? What bad times are? I grew up in a tenement in New York. My mother, my father and eleven kids in one and a half rooms – *(He suddenly gets an itch on his chest; he scratches himself.)* – we had two beds and a cot, you had to take a number off the wall to go to sleep – *(The other side of his chest itches. He scratches it.)* – my father was five foot three, weighed a hundred and twenty-seven pounds – *(His back itches. He tries to scratch it.)* what the hell is that?

LIPTON. Can't get to it, can you? ...They can put an itch on your back, a *gorilla* couldn't reach it.

JOE. Do what you want. Bankrupt me, freeze me, tear out my insides – *(Tries to get at his back again.)* oh, God, that's driving me crazy. *(Turns his back toward* LIPTON.*)* Could you just scratch me for a minute? ...Nobody would know.

LIPTON. Certainly. Bend over. I'll scratch while you sign the paper.

JOE. *No!* No, I'm not signing anything! Oh! I'd trade my entire hand for one ten-inch finger.

LIPTON. Have the bottoms of your feet started to itch yet?

JOE. *(Scratching his back.)* No. Not yet... Now! Now – they just started! *(He flops down on the floor and rips his shoes off, frantically scratching the soles of his feet.)* Ohh! Oh, that's worse than the back... I'd rather have all my teeth pulled out than have my feet itch.

LIPTON. That's scheduled for Thursday... Now it starts in-between the fingers.

JOE. Oh, it's in-between the fingers now. *(Tries to scratch in-between his fingers, the soles of his feet and his back.)* I can't scratch everywhere at once. I need another arm.

LIPTON. *(Observing him.)* When it starts to itch in your crotch, I'm leaving.

JOE. *(Scratching everywhere.)* I expected pain but this is torture... Oh, it's in the nostrils now. Now it's up the nose!

> *(He scratches nose.)*

LIPTON. *(Turns away, shields his eyes.)* I'll miss *that* one, if you don't mind! ...Give in, Joe.

> *(**JOE** keeps scratching.)*

JOE. He's my God. He gave me life and my life meaning. I will not renounce Him. *(Grabs his shoulder in sudden pain.)* Oh! Oh, what's that?

LIPTON. Neuralgia – with a side order of bursitis... Joe, listen to me... *Nobody* believes any more. The Church is thinking of closing two days a week... Synagogues are selling tickets for the High Holidays at a discount.

JOE. *(Grabs other arm.)* Ogghhhhhhhhhhh! Oggghhhh! Never, never... What is that?

LIPTON. Tennis elbow.

JOE. Aggghhhhhhh! Get out! Get out and let me suffer alone. Let me bear my pain alone.

LIPTON. Who's looking to stay? This is not my idea of *That's Entertainment. (He puts the papers back into his briefcase.)* Well, Benjy-Boy, what we've got here is a stalemate.

JOE. *(Scratching, stomping, writhing – he is being attacked everywhere at once.)* Agghhhh! Ogghhhh! It's itching again. Everything and everywhere is itching me. Do something. Help me! Isn't there something you can do?

LIPTON. If I could, I would. You think I have no feelings? You think I like to see people suffer? I *hate* this job... If only I could get a good Carvel franchise near Miami, I would get out in a minute.

JOE. Uggghhhhhhhhhhhh!

LIPTON. I'm going. Try not to scream until I'm gone. I'm getting nauseous.

JOE. A doctor! Get me a doctor, please...

LIPTON. Don't ask for doctors. They can't help you and they'll charge you a fortune. Think it over, Joe. If it gets worse...you've got my number.

JOE. Agggghhhhhhh! That's the worst one. What is that?

LIPTON. That, Joe is hemorrhoids. Goodbye!

(He opens the French door and leaps over the balcony railing.)

(Curtain.)

ACT II

(It is a few days later. The house is gone – burnt to the ground. Parts of the brick walls are still standing, but the roof and wooden-beamed ceilings are no more. Some of the burnt timbers can still be seen on the ground of the "former" living room, where they have crashed during the fire. We can see the sky. It is a cold, bleak, overcast day. Smoke still rises from the smoldering ruins. The furniture has been crushed and burnt. There is very little left worth saving.)

*(Through the portals which once were the entrance from the dining room, and where one charred oak door hangs precariously from a hinge, come **MORRIS** and **MADY**. Their clothes are tattered and singed. They enter the room listlessly, **MADY** carries a Gucci shopping bag. **MORRIS** carries a broom and dustpan. They step over debris and twisted furniture.)*

MADY. *(Looks around at the charred ruins.)* Well, I tell you one thing – I ain't cleanin' up *this* mess.

MORRIS. *(Morosely.)* Well, you got to look on the bright side, Mady... At least we only got *one* floor to do now.

MADY. Never seen a fire spread so fast in all my life. This house got "well done" quicker than a barbecued chicken.

MORRIS. It was the wind. Came up outa nowhere blowin' fire every which ways. *(Points off.)* Looka that! First time I ever seen a swimming pool burn down.

MADY. Now, how come the fire department never answered the alarm? And how come no neighbors bothered comin' over here to help us? And how come when it started to rain, it rained everywhere but right here? I ain't a gamblin' woman, Morris, but somehow I got the feelin' this family has "crapped out"!

MORRIS. *(Stops; thinks.)* You think it's true, Mady?

MADY. What's that?

MORRIS. That the Lord is testin' Mr. Benjamin? That it's God who's burned us and froze us and starvin' us just to see if Mr. Benjamin really loves Him the way he say he do?

MADY. I hope so. Sure would be a waste if all this misery was nothin' but misery. What time is it?

MORRIS. What difference does it make around here? *(Looks at his watch.)* Uh-oh. Get ready. It's time for Mr. Benjamin to be gettin' up now. Hold on.

> *(From the distance we hear a scream – a long, agonizing scream. It is so painful and mournful, it hardly sounds human. It dies slowly,* **MADY** *and* **MORRIS** *have been looking back in the direction of that horrible sound.)*

MADY. He sounds a little better today.

MORRIS. He ain't gettin' better. He just ain't *screamin'* as good.

ROSE. *(Offstage.)* Morris? Mady? Are you in the living room?

MORRIS. It's Mrs. Benjamin. *(Calls out.)* Yes, ma'am, here we are. We're outside in the house.

> *(***ROSE*** *and* ***SARAH*** *straggle in through the "portal.")*

ROSE. Oh, I'm so glad you're both home. I forgot my key.

MORRIS. *(Getting up to help her.)* Careful, Mrs. Benjamin. Lotta that furniture is still hot.

ROSE. Look at my beautiful house...my beautiful living room... And we just had the windows done.

*(**ROSE** and **SARAH** climb over the rubble.)*

SARAH. You're tired. Mother. Why don't you sit down and rest?

MORRIS. Set yourself here, Mrs. Benjamin. I think it used to be the sofa.

*(**ROSE** sits down.)*

Would you like a carrot to chew on, Mrs. Benjamin?

ROSE. No thanks, Morris. I don't want to spoil my dinner.

MADY. You won't, 'cause that's it.

ROSE. *(Looks around sadly.)* You know, Mady, when I was young I always wanted a big house with a little fireplace... Now I've got a big fireplace with a little house.

MORRIS. If you need to borrow some money, Mrs. Benjamin, we'll be glad to help you out.

ROSE. You're both so kind... Did I tell you that David is gone?

SARAH. He drank a whole bottle of brandy and ran out blind drunk. Ben went out looking for him.

ROSE. Don't say anything to Mr. Benjamin. He's got enough on his mind now. If only David were here. He keeps asking for David. "Where is my little David?" he says... over and over through his chapped lips.

MORRIS. Listen. Someone's comin'.

ROSE. Oh, dear. And the place is a mess.

MORRIS. It's Mr. Ben.

BEN. *(Rushing in.)* He's coming! Daddy's coming!

ROSE. Everybody, clear all this debris away. He has to be very careful where he steps. Over there. Put it over there.

> *(They all start to move a large beam to make a path. They move it to the other side of the room.)*

MADY. The Walls of Jericho – that's what we got here is the Walls of Jericho.

(They put it down.)

ROSE. *(Looks at it.)* No, it looks terrible there... Never mind.

BEN. Here he comes.

ROSE. Now, remember, don't touch him. His skin is *very* sensitive. Nobody touch him, please.

> *(They all turn to the doorway,* **JOE** *stands there, leaning on a stick. He is bent over, half in pain, half because of an aging process that has made him old before his time. Even his hair has grayed. He is in tatters and rags, cloths wrapped around his feet. He is parched, shriveled and weak. His lips are cracked, and when he speaks, it is with great effort and pain.)*

JOE. Ail... Ail in hoo...

MORRIS. What's that, Mr. Benjamin?

JOE. Ail... Ail in hoo...

ROSE. It hurts him to speak. His lips get stuck together. What are you trying to say, dear?

JOE. Ail in hoo...

ROSE. A nail in your shoe?

JOE. Ail in hoo...hurts!

ROSE. Poor Joe.

JOE. Daba?

ROSE. What, dear?

JOE. Daba? ...Bear daba?

ROSE. Where's David? I don't know, dear. David's gone.

JOE. Daba gobe?

ROSE. Yes. You mustn't worry. He'll be all right... You must take care of *yourself* now, Joe.

JOE. *(Turns away sorrowfully.)* Daba's gobe...

MORRIS. Well, it's good to see you up and about again, Mr. Benjamin.

MADY. Dinner's gonna be ready soon, Mr. Benjamin. We're havin' pot luck tonight.

(*JOE seems to be sagging.*)

MORRIS. You shouldn't be standin' like that, Mr. Benjamin. (*Moves toward him.*) Let me help you sit.

JOE. (*Panicked, backs away.*) Nah! Nah!

ROSE. (*Screams.*) Don't touch him!

MORRIS. I won't! I won't touch him!

ROSE. You mustn't touch him!

MORRIS. I'm not going to touch you, Mr. Benjamin.

JOE. Dow tuch... Dow tuch... Muzzzn tuch...

ROSE. No one is going to touch you, dear. We know how your skin feels.

JOE. Ha! ...Ski fees ha!

ROSE. Skin feels hot. We know, darling.

SARAH. (*Sobs.*) Oh, Daddy. Poor Daddy!

MADY. He needs his strength, that's what he needs... You want a nice carrot, Mr. Benjamin?

JOE. Ka-hoo!

MADY. What?

JOE. Ka-hoo!

ROSE. He can't chew.

MORRIS. You want something to drink?

JOE. Ka-swa!

ROSE. He can't swallow.

SARAH. Isn't there *anything* we can do, Daddy?

JOE. Ka-thi!

ROSE. He can't think of anything.

JOE. (*Looks around.*) Gow... Evthi gow...

ROSE. Everything's gone? No, Joe. Not everything. We still have each other. We're still alive and together, Joe.

JOE. Evthi gow – in here! (*He indicates his heart by pointing to it. His finger touches his chest and it sets off an agonizing pain.*) AaaaaagggggggHHHHHH!!!

ROSE. *Don't touch it, Joe*, just point to it.

SARAH. *(Turns away.)* Poor Daddy.

    *(She buries herself in **BEN**'s arms.)*

JOE. Away... Take away...

    (He is forming his words a little better by now.)

ROSE. They're your children, Joe. They love you.

SARAH. We're not leaving you, Daddy.

BEN. We're sticking, Dad, even if the pain gets worse.

JOE. *Worse?* Worse than this? *(He shakes head.)* No. There's no worse. This is it!

ROSE. That's right, Joe. Things are going to get better, you'll see. David will come home soon and we'll build the house up again and we'll find a nice skin lotion for you. Everything will be all right, Joe. I know it will. We love you, Joe.

JOE. And I...love you.

    *(**ROSE**, filled with love and compassion, rushes to **JOE** and takes him in her arms.)*

ROSE. Oh, Joe!

JOE. AGGGGHHHHHHHHHH!

ROSE. *(Backs off.)* Oh, I'm sorry, darling!

JOE. Dow tuch... Dow tuch!

ROSE. No. I won't touch you again, Joe. No.

MADY. *(Gets on her knees.)* Oh, Lord, help this poor man in his sufferin'...

MORRIS. *(On his knees.)* Amen!

MADY. Help this poor man through his pain.

MORRIS. Amen!

MADY. Help this poor man in his anguish!

MORRIS. Amen!

ROSE. Joe, isn't that sweet? They're praying for you... And it's their day off.

JOE. Thank...you.

MADY. Everybody pray. Everybody down on their knees to God.

(They all start to kneel, including **JOE.***)*

NOT YOU, MR. BENJAMIN!

*(***JOE** *stops.)*

ROSE. We'll do it, Joe. We'll pray for you.

(He gets up, then nods to them.)

JOE. Okay.

MADY. If you hear us, Lord, give us a sign. Make it known in our hearts, Lord, that you hear us.

MORRIS. Make it known.

MADY. Make it known in our souls, Lord, that you hear us.

BEN. Make it known.

MADY. Make it known in our ears, Lord, that you hear us.

JOE. *(Loud but not clear.)* May it knowwww...

MADY. Everybody!

ALL. Amen, Lord!

JOE. Amen, Lord! Oh, I bit my tongue!

(He cries.)

ROSE. Oh, dear God, his tongue is swelling up. Look at it. He doesn't have enough room in his mouth.

JOE. Arrrggghhhhhh!

SARAH. *(Sobs.)* Oh, Daddy. Poor Daddy.

MORRIS. *(On his knees, pounds the floor with his fist.)* Poor Mr. Benjamin. Poor Mr. Benjamin. Poor Mr. Benjamin. *(Accidentally hits* **JOE***'s foot.)* I'm sorry. I'm sorry. I'm sorry.

BEN. When's all this gonna be over?

SARAH. When, Mother, when?

ROSE. *(Defiantly.)* When? ...Now! That's right, I said "Now!" ...I've had enough, Joe. We've *all* had enough. I want my David back. I want my house back. I want your tongue to go down... Make it stop, Joe. Please make it stop.

JOE. *(With difficulty.)* There'th nothing I can do... I can't thtop it...

ROSE. *(Screams.)* DON'T TELL ME THERE'S NOTHING YOU CAN DO! You *know* what you can do. You can stop it all, Joe, with three little words. You can end our pain, our misery... Say it, Joe. Say it, and we can all go to bed and watch some television. Please...

(She breaks down sobbing.)

JOE. Don't... Don't ask me, Rose...

ROSE. I'm not asking, I'm *begging*!

JOE. Don't beg me, Rose.

ROSE. Then I *demand*! I *demand*, Joe Benjamin, that you give up your precious God. How can you love someone who makes us suffer so much?

JOE. David makes me suffer...and I love him.

ROSE. That's different. He'll grow out of it. But God is millions of years old – He should know better! I believed before, Joe... When I was a little girl... When I met you... When we had the children... But not now. Not when I see what He's doing to you. He's not nice, Joe. If you don't renounce Him, Joe...then I'm going to renounce *you*!

SARAH. Mother!

JOE. I can't help myself... I love my God...

ROSE. *(Angrily.)* Why couldn't you just have a mistress like other men?

JOE. I'm sorry, Rose... Forgive me...

ROSE. Then stay here and suffer – because *I'm* going. I've got five mouths to feed. If there *is* a God, that's what He intended *me* to do... I'm going to Welcome Wagon and get some coffee and doughnuts. Come, everybody.

BEN. You mean leave Dad here like this?

SARAH. We can't leave him alone, Mother. He'll die!

ROSE. He won't die. God doesn't want him to die. He wants him to stay here and suffer for a hundred and twenty years. Then they'll *both* be happy. We'll be dead and buried, and your father will be sitting on porcupine needles... Have a good time, Joe. Come, children.

BEN. All right. We'll go. But as soon as I know the others are all right, I'm coming back. I'm not David. Goodbye, Dad...and good luck. *(And without thinking, he grabs* **JOE***'s hand to shake it – then realizes his mistake.)* That hurts, doesn't it?

> *(***JOE*** nods quietly.)*

Sorry about that.

SARAH. Goodbye, Daddy.

JOE. Sarah... One kiss... One goodbye kiss.

SARAH. But if I touch you –

JOE. A kiss from you could never hurt.

> *(***SARAH*** bends down and kisses his cheek gently.)*

That's the first time I felt good in three days. Button your coat.

> *(***SARAH*** bursts into tears and runs to* **BEN**. *Both leave.)*

ROSE. Come. It's getting late. With our luck, there'll be a transit strike. Goodbye, Joe.

JOE. *(Stopping her.)* Rosey!

ROSE. You haven't called me Rosey in thirty years.

JOE. Take care, Rosey...and try and forgive me.

ROSE. It was such a nice house. We were all so happy here... Why couldn't God have tested a young couple with a small apartment? *(She cries.)* I love you, Joe... I forgive you.

> *(And she runs off. Only* **MADY** *and* **MORRIS** *remain, standing together.)*

JOE. What are you waiting for? Go!

MORRIS. We want to stay with *you*, Mr. Benjamin.

JOE. What does a suffering man living all alone in ashes need two in help for? Go with Mrs. Benjamin, Morris. She needs you.

MADY. I have a sister who can come in two days a week...

JOE. Thank you both and God bless you.

MADY. Just "Thank you" will be plenty, Mr. Benjamin.

MORRIS. May the Lord have mercy on his painful soul.

MADY. Hallelujah – and let's get the hell outa here!

> *(They are gone,* **JOE** *is alone. He crawls to the sofa in great pain and sits. Then he looks upward.)*

JOE. Okay, God. What's next? ...What's next, God?

> *(Suddenly there is a crack of thunder,* **JOE** *winces. Then we hear a deep, rich, resonant voice – as if from the heavens.)*

VOICE. Joe...

JOE. What?

VOICE. Joseph Melvin Benjamin! This – is your God!

JOE. *(Leans forward, excited.)* God? ...Is it really you, God?

VOICE. Didn't I just say it was? ...Of all the creatures on this earth you are My favorite, Joe. I love you more than the birds and the butterflies and the crocodiles and the cockroaches...especially the cockroaches.

JOE. *(Bowing his head.)* Oh, thank you, Lord...

VOICE. Your test is over.

JOE. *(With great relief.)* Ohhh!

VOICE. You have met the challenge of faith and have emerged triumphant... I love thee as thou loves thine... And thee will be rewarded as thou would wish thine to reward thee...

JOE. Thank Thee, My Lord.

VOICE. Raise thyself to be blessed, Joseph.

> *(***JOE*** does.)*

Knowing now that thy test is over, say the words just for Me... As a final tribute of thy love for Me, Joseph, say what thou couldst not say before. Say it, Joseph, say "I renounce God."

JOE. *(Puzzled.)* What?

VOICE. It's all right. The test is over... It couldn't hurt, Joe.

JOE. What is this? ...It's a trick. That's what it is! It's a trick, isn't it?

VOICE. It is not a trick. God does not trick. God is a busy man. Say it, Joe. Say it before I get upset.

JOE. A trick... That voice... I know that voice... It's not God! It's *you,* isn't it?

VOICE. It's not me. It's God, I'm telling you. Why would I lie? I'm God, I'm telling you, *I'M GOD! I'M GOD! I'M GOD!*

> *(And as "God's" voice booms out, the fireplace collapses...and standing behind it holding a cordless microphone is* **SIDNEY LIPTON**. *He turns around and looks at* **JOE** *sheepishly – caught in the act much as the Wizard of Oz was by Dorothy.)*

LIPTON. *(Smiles and speaks into the microphone.)* April Fool!

JOE. I knew it! I knew that voice!

LIPTON. Tell the truth, did I fool you? Heh? *(Does his "God" voice.)* Joseph Benjamin, this is your God. *(Regular voice again.)* They hired me once to do that in a temple on Eighty-eighth and Park – I raised over a hundred thousand dollars in donations.

JOE. Leave me alone today, please. Besides suffering, I'm not feeling well.

LIPTON. *(Looks around.)* I don't blame you. Look at this place... If you don't get the screens up, you're going to have one buggy summer.

JOE. If I've lost everything else, why can't I lose you too?

LIPTON. Can I make a suggestion about the furniture? ...Try Lemon Pledge. Rub it in for about six years and let it dry.

JOE. You're gloating, aren't you? You think you've won. You think you've beaten me. Well, you're wrong. You're wasting your time, Lipton. All I wait for now is my death.

LIPTON. Death? You got a long wait. You got fifty, sixty years of healthy suffering in front of you yet. What are you talking about? You're in the prime of pain... Oh, by the way, I brought the list with me.

(He takes a sheet of paper out of his pocket.)

JOE. What list?

LIPTON. The previews. The coming attractions. Let me read you what's playing July tenth through August fourteenth... *(Reads.)* A hernia, gastritis, a double impacted wisdom tooth, a root canal job, the heartbreak of psoriasis, constipation, diarrhea, piles, dysentery, chills, fever, athlete's foot, lumbago, a touch of gonorrhea and a general feeling of loginess... All this, mind you, is on the left side of your body.

JOE. If I'm alive I'll endure.

LIPTON. "I'll endure." I've heard that before. Would you like to know who renounced God today, Joe? If I told you who renounced God today you would be shocked. I couldn't believe it when I heard it.

JOE. I don't care.

LIPTON. Detroit. The entire city of Detroit renounced... including three hundred tourists just passing through.

JOE. I am what God made me.

LIPTON. And stop talking like you're Moses. You are not Moses. Moses was a big star. You're lucky God even pays attention to you.

JOE. I am an infinitesimal speck on the eyelash of the universe...but God sees me.

LIPTON. With binoculars, maybe. Vain, that's what you are – vain, self-centered and a swellhead. Who do you think you are to take up God's time like this? Do you know something? This will be the first time in nineteen years that he misses the Christmas show at Radio City Music Hall. And for what? Look at you! A mess... Walking around in a burnt bathrobe and that *fekokta* stick. You look like a shepherd for the Salvation Army. I didn't want to mention it before – *(He whispers.)* – lately you don't smell too good either.

    (He puts his scarf to his nose.)

JOE. It won't work, Sidney. No matter what you say, it won't work.

LIPTON. I hate this job. I can't take it any more. I'm having a nervous breakdown... Why doesn't God help me? Why should you be the favorite?

JOE. I'm sorry, Sidney. Forgive me... How can I help you?

LIPTON. If you won't renounce God, then – then will – will you –

JOE. Will I what, Sidney? Ask me.

LIPTON. Will you give me a letter of recommendation? I've been fired!

    (He opens his coat – the "G" has been taken off his football jersey.)

JOE. Oh, Sidney, don't tell me. I'm so sorry.

LIPTON. God laid off fourteen hundred people today. Everyone went – messengers, angels, bishops, Hebrew-school teachers... I saw two Cardinals trying to get jobs at Chock Full O'Nuts... It's because of inflation... Do you know what red velvet slippers cost today? ...I haven't even told Sylvia yet.

JOE. She sounds like a good woman. She'll understand.

LIPTON. There goes our dream of Florida. You know how far south Sylvia has been in her life? ...Canal Street... not even the downtown side.

JOE. Then why did you come here today?

LIPTON. *(Shrugs.)* I was hoping I could change your mind... If I could get this account, they might reconsider.

JOE. God loves you, Sidney – he'll provide.

LIPTON. He wouldn't even say hello to me in the hallway... What am I going to do now? I'm forty-four years old – it's a little late in life to take up pro-football.

JOE. We must carry whatever burdens God gives us.

LIPTON. Sure. The poor carry their burdens and the rich have them delivered. Where's the justice? ...Well, I don't care any more... What could He do to me now? *(Yells up.)* Hey, God! Do You hear me? ...*I renounce You, God!*

JOE. *(Yells.)* NO! DON'T DO THAT!

LIPTON. *(Yells up again.)* I give You up, God! Thanks for nothing. The *Devil* cares more about people. At least *he* entertains them... *The Exorcist* grossed over a hundred and thirty million dollars – domestic!

JOE. Take it back, Sidney.

LIPTON. *(Yells up.)* Hey, God, You hear me? May You have the same lousy weather You give *us* every year... especially Labor Day weekend.

JOE. We all have our own tests to go through, Sidney...

LIPTON. Why did *you* have to be mine? Even *you* couldn't take you, believe me. *(Sobs.)* What have I done?

JOE. Shh... Shh... It's all right, Sidney.

LIPTON. Tell Him I'm sorry, Joe. He knows you, He likes you... You, He'll listen to. Tell Him not to forsake me.

JOE. Of course I'll tell Him, Sidney. He won't...shh...

LIPTON. *(Wipes his eyes on his sleeve.)* Thank you, Joseph. I have to go now... I have an interview at two o'clock with United Parcel.

(He stops suddenly; looks around.)

JOE. Good luck, Sidney.

LIPTON. Shh! Listen!

JOE. What is it?

LIPTON. I hear something. Someone's out there…

JOE. Where? I can't see.

(He still can't move around freely.)

LIPTON. *(Points.)* There! There, did you see it move?

JOE. See what? Where should I look? There's nothing out there but smoke and ashes.

LIPTON. And a bush… See that one bush over there? It's still burning a little on the bottom… There's someone behind there.

JOE. Behind the burning bush?

LIPTON. *(Stops; looks at JOE.)* Did you hear what you just said?

JOE. What did I say?

LIPTON. Behind the burning bush… Anything strike you familiar about that phrase?

JOE. What are you saying?

LIPTON. Nothing.

(He backs away.)

JOE. What are you implying?

LIPTON. Nothing… But don't ask me what I'm thinking.

JOE. Do you mean – ?

LIPTON. I doubt it. He never makes house calls. But with you, who knows?

JOE. Oh, my God.

LIPTON. *(Nods.)* It's possible. Your test isn't over yet, Joe… Maybe He's going for a big finish… This is no place for me. Goodbye, Joe.

JOE. *NO!* Stay! Help me!

LIPTON. Hold out. Whatever they do to you now, hold out another few minutes… Keep saying you love God, and Monday morning you'll be back in the box business, Joe.

JOE. I'm not *interested* in the box business any more.

LIPTON. Don't turn it down. I could run it for you. I'm available.

(*He starts exiting through the fireplace.*)

JOE. Don't leave me now. I need you. Help me, Sidney...

LIPTON. Goodbye, Joe. Good luck... If you think of it, get me an autograph.

(*And he is gone, **JOE** is alone. He is unable to move with any facility, and whatever movement he does make is still painful. Add to this his immeasurable fear of what may be out there for him... We hear a wind come up. It almost sounds like a voice wailing.*)

JOE. Who's out there? ...Tell me who's there, please. I'm frightened. Is it – is it who I think it is? ...Why don't You say something? ...What more do You want of me? ...Say *something* to me, PLEASE.

(*A clap of thunder is heard. A shaft of light beams a single ray... And suddenly someone appears standing in the ray. It is **DAVID**. He looks in **JOE**'s direction, but not directly at him.*)

JOE. David.

DAVID. (*He turns back, waves.*) Thanks for the lift.

(*A car horn honks; then the sound of it driving away.*)

What's for dinner? I smell charcoal.

JOE. David, David, it's you!

(*He reaches out for him.*)

DAVID. We haven't had a cookout in years... Ah, a special occasion! Can I have a drink, Dad?

JOE. (*Arms extended.*) David, help me. Come here, David... I've been so worried for you.

DAVID. Well, as you can see, I'm fine... (*Falls over a beam.*) And how is the family? ...Mother, you seem so quiet tonight.

JOE. What are you talking about? Your mother's not here... Can't you see they're all gone?

DAVID. Really? Mady too? ...Morris, are you there?

JOE. What's wrong with you? Are you drunk again? ...You're dead drunk, aren't you?

DAVID. Not *dead* drunk, Dad. Blind drunk. The only problem is... I'm not drunk any more.

> *(He steps into the room and feels around... We realize he is stone blind.)*

JOE. Oh, God... Oh, my God! *(He tries to reach out for* **DAVID***, then looks up to the sky.)* What have You done to my boy? What have You done to my David?

DAVID. Who are you talking to? Who came in, Dad?

JOE. *(Upward.)* God, how could You do such a thing?

DAVID. Oh, *Him*? ...Still on that, are we?

JOE. *(Clenches his fists and shakes them at the heavens. His grief, his anger, is enormous.)* Is this Your work? ...Is this Your test of faith and love? ...You blind my first-born son and still expect me to love you? Punish *me*, not him! Blind *me*, not my son... Where is your love? Your compassion? Your justice? ...I AM ANGRY AT YOU, GOD! REALLY, REALLY ANGRY! ...And *STILL* I don't renounce you! How do you like *that*, God?

> *(There is a bolt of lightning and a crack of thunder.* **DAVID** *cries out and holds his eyes, then takes his hands away.)*

DAVID. *(Lightly.)* I think that did it, Pop!

JOE. You can see, David? *(***DAVID** *nods,* **JOE** *looks up.)* It's over. The test is over! Oh, thank you, God. Thank you! ...I'm sorry I lost my temper – but after all, I'm only human. You don't know what it's like... Try it sometime.

ROSE. *(Offstage.)* Joe? ...Joe, are you all right?

JOE. In here, Rose! We're in here.

> *(***ROSE** *appears carrying two huge shopping bags of food.)*

ROSE. I've come back, Joe. I couldn't leave you... Oh, David's home. I was so worried... Did you tell him, Joe?

JOE. Tell him what?

ROSE. That the house burned down? ...Never mind. *(Hands* **DAVID** *packages.)* Here, David, look for the kitchen.

>   *(He goes out.)*

> I have *food,* Joe. Where is everybody – Mady? Morris? Come on, we're all waiting.

>   *(They all come in.)*

SARAH. Look, Daddy, *food!*

JOE. Where did you get it?

ROSE. I won it on a TV game show. It started to rain, and we all ducked into this building... I didn't know it was a television studio... They picked me out of the audience. And today they had a new game where each contestant gets a celebrity helper and both of you have to help each other. And the category I picked was famous Biblical stories, and we got every question right... And do you know who the celebrity was who helped me, Joe?

JOE. *(Looks slightly upward.)* Yes, Rose... I think I know.

ROSE. Don Rickles... He was as sweet as can be.

MADY. Oh, it's so good to see you looking well, Mr. Benjamin.

>   *(***DAVID** *reenters.)*

DAVID. Hi.

SARAH. David! I'm so glad you're home... I think a man followed me on the streets... He just kept looking me up and down, up and down.

DAVID. No one's going to look you up and down. Button your coat.

JOE. You hear? Isn't it wonderful? Mady, Morris... Look at David now. *That's* my son.

MADY. We all know who he is, Mr. Benjamin.

ROSE. Come on everybody, into the kitchen. We're going to have a fat, juicy butterball turkey for dinner.

(They all start to go except **DAVID**. **JOE** *is the last leaving.)*

JOE. *(Turning back.)* Are you coming, David?

DAVID. In a minute, Dad... I just want to try and clean up around here.

JOE. Are you sure you're all right, David?

DAVID. I'm fine, Dad... Thank God.

JOE. *(Nods, smiles.)* I'd go through it all again, David, just to hear you say that.

(He goes out. **DAVID** *is alone. He starts to clean up, then turns and looks up to God.)*

DAVID. Okay, God... If you got room for one more, count me in... I just wanted to thank you for sparing my father's life... That's all I wanted to say... Amen.

VOICE. *(Offstage.)* Amen!

DAVID. *(Turns.)* Who said that?

LIPTON. *(Appears.)* Don't worry, it's not who you're thinking... I wonder if I could talk to you for a minute, young man... Guess who's absolutely crazy about you?

(Curtain.)

COSTUME PLOT

Joe:

Act I – Scene One:
　　pajamas, bathrobe, slippers

Cold Scene – Scene Two:
　　sweater, pants, shoes in galoshes, brown socks, scarf, coat with fur
　　　collar, fur hat, gloves, handkerchief in pocket, carrying napkin

Act II:
　　black socks, black shoes, burnt pants, burnt thermal shirt, burnt
　　　jacket, burnt bathrobe with tie belt

Rose:

Act I – Scene One:
　　nightgown, robe, slippers, hose, jewelry, handkerchief

Cold Scene – Scene Two:
　　tee shirt, brown skirt, brown suede boots, mink coat, fox hat, gloves,
　　　some jewelry

Act II:
　　tee shirts, brown skirt, burnt boots, burnt mink coat, burnt fox hat,
　　　burnt gloves, burnt handkerchief

Sidney:

Act I – Scene One:
　　beige pants, tee shirt, black socks, brown hushpuppy shoes, scarf,
　　　cap, raincoat, wrist watch, red tee shirt G

Cold Scene – Scene Two:
　　second raincoat with smoke pocket, red tee shirt, beige pants, Hush
　　　Puppy shoes, scarf, cap

Act II:
　　first raincoat, red tee shirt without G, beige pants, scarf, cap

David:

Act I – Scene One:
　　jeans, sneakers (no socks), evening shirt, evening vest, evening
　　　jacket, bow tie, trench coat, party hat

Cold Scene – Scene Two:
　　lumber jacket, jeans, tee shirt, two scarves, football helmet, gloves,
　　　blanket

Act II:
　　tee shirt, burnt lumber jacket, jeans, tennis shoes, black velour

Mady:

Act I – Scene One:
    hose, night gown, robe, slippers, turban

Cold Scene – Scene *Two:*
    maids dress and apron, good coat, hat, maids cap, boots, gloves

Act II:
    maids burnt dress, burnt coat, burnt apron over coat, burnt hat,
    burnt gloves, burnt boots, burnt handkerchief, burnt maids cap
    over hat

Morris:

Act I – Scene One:
    tee shirt, pajamas, robe, slippers, black socks

Cold Scene – Scene Two:
    ear muffs, overcoat, white shirt, white waiters coat, black bow tie,
    dark grey pants, gloves, hunting boots

Act II:
    burnt overcoat, burnt boots, burnt pants, turtleneck sweater, burnt
    ear muffs, burnt gloves

Sarah:

Act I – Scene One:
    red wig, night gown, robe, barefooted

Cold Scene – Scene Two:
    red wig, boots, jeans, tee shirt, parka, scarf, gloves, hat

Act II:
    red wig, burnt jeans, tee shirt, burnt sweater, burnt parka, burnt
    hat, burnt gloves

Ben:

Act I – Scene One:
    red wig, pajamas, robe, slippers

Cold Scene – Scene Two:
    red wig, tee shirt, black socks, cowboy boots, tan parka, scarf, hat,
    jeans, gloves

Act II:
    red wig, tee shirt, jeans, burnt parka, burnt hat, sweater burnt,
    burnt gloves

PROPERTY LIST

Pre-Set:

Offstage left:

   jewel box with jewels (**Rose**) Act I, Scene One
   tall glass ¼ full with Swizzle Stick (**David**) Act I, Scene One
   11 bags with food
         3 of them shopping bags Act II
   pole (**Joe**) Act II

Offstage right:

   silver tray (**Morris**) Act I, Scene Two
   napkin (**Joe**) Act I, Scene Two
   black velour (**Lipton**) Act I, Scene One *(To cover actor as he gets into place behind sofa.)*
   dust pan & broom (**Morris**) Act II
   Gucci shopping bag (**Mady**) Act II
   dust rags (**Mady**) Act II
   feather duster (**Mady**) Act II

PERSONAL PROPS

Lipton:

attache case – Act I, Scene Two
In Case:

   3 sets of papers
   steno pad
   rubber stamp
   2 Bic Banana

watch – Act I, Scene Two
hernia list – Act II Joe Benjamin List – Act I, Scene One
pack with speaker – Act II

David:

paper hat (party hat)
helmet

Morris:

pocket watch

Act I, Scene I:
Set:

   deck washed
   door stop stage left
   bar
         silver dish with ice
         decanters

soda spritzer
glasses
Chivas Regal bottle – cap on tight, under bar upstage
crystal vase *(downstage end of bar on lower shelf)*
sofa table
telephone
dish sofa pillows (2)
rug (downstage right corner not tacked down)
picture of Mother on fireplace
bench
chair (downstage left)
end table (downstage left)
pedestal with bust
eye glasses (out on terrace) (**Lipton**)
upstage center doors closed
stage right door closed
stage left doors closed

Act I, Scene Two:
soda spritzer (back to bar)
sofa pillow (back to sofa)
flip pictures stage right and stage left
open upstage center doors
stage right and stage left doors closed

Strike:
bench
arm chair
table
crystal vase (from sofa table)
dish (from sofa table)
2 Chinese vases (from under bar)

Set:
place wooden box in place of table and arm chair downstage left

Act II:
Set:
rug (burned)
big beam
sofa (burned)
golf trophy (in fireplace)
no rocks in fireplace
Mother's picture on fireplace
large spoon downstage right
salt & pepper downstage right
burnt timbers

Printed in the USA
CPSIA information can be obtained
at www.ICGtesting.com
JSHW011924101224
75169JS00015B/49